THE STUDENT-ATHLETE & COLLEGE RECRUITING

Twenty-Seventh Printing

Rick Wire

Athletic Guide Publishing

THE STUDENT-ATHLETE
&
COLLEGE RECRUITING

By Rick Wire

Published by:

Athletic Guide Publishing
PO Box 1050
Flagler Beach, FL 32136-1050 USA
386.439.2050
athleticguidepublishing@gmail.com

Copyright © 1998, 1999, 2000, 2001, 2002, 2003, 2004, 2005, 2006, 2007, 2008, 2009, 2010, 2011, 2012, 2013, 2014, 2015, 2016, 2017, 2018, 2019 & 2020

by Rick Wire

First printing 1998
Second printing 1999, completely revised
Third printing 2000, completely revised
Fourth printing January 2001, completely revised
Fifth printing July 2001, completely revised
Sixth printing August 2002, completely revised
Seventh printing October 2003, completely revised
Eighth printing July 2004, completely revised
Ninth printing June 2005, completely revised
Tenth printing June 2006, completely revised
Eleventh printing June 2007, completely revised
Twelfth printing June 2008, completely revised
Thirteenth printing August 2009, completely revised
Fourteenth printing August 2010, completely revised
Fifteenth printing August 2011, completely revised
Sixteenth printing August 2012, completely revised
Seventeenth printing June 2013, completely revised
Eighteenth printing June 2014, completely revised
Nineteenth printing October 2015, completely revised
Twentieth printing August 2016, completely revised
Twenty-First printing January 2017, completely revised
Twenty-Second printing October 2017, completely revised
Twenty-Third printing September 2018, completely revised
Twenty-Fourth printing January 2019, completely revised
Twenty-Fifth printing October 2019, completely revised
Twenty-Sixth printing December 2019, completely revised
Twenty-Seventh printing January 2020, completely revised

Publisher's Cataloging-in-Publication Data

Wire, Rick 1955-

>   The Student-Athlete & College Recruiting / by Rick Wire,

>   141p. - 14x22 cm.

ISBN 10: 1-880941-86-4 / ISBN 13: 978-1-880941-86-7   (pbk.)

1. college reference - recruiting, scholarships, NCAA regulations I. title

All NCAA references in this publication are based upon the NCAA Manual and portions of the NCAA Guide for the College-Bound-Student-Athlete have been reprinted in this book with permission of the NCAA. Direct inquiries regarding NCAA regulations to:

NCAA
PO Box 6222
Indianapolis, IN 46206-6222

317.917.6222
For a free copy of the NCAA College Bound Student-Athlete Guide call:
NCAA 800.638.3731

For additional information regarding the NCAA, review their internet site at www.ncaa.org

Dynamite Sports
1284 N. Middleton Road
Carlisle, PA 17013
717.554.4950 (cell)
www.dynamitesports.com
rwire@dynamitesports.com (email)

Athletic Guide Publishing
PO Box 1050
Flagler Beach, FL 32136
386.439.2050
athleticguidepublishing@gmail.com

Acknowledgement

The Student-Athlete and College Recruiting is dedicated to my mom, Shirley. When I was ten years old my father, who was an alcoholic, left us. Mom raised me, my brother, and two sisters by herself. As a parent, I now know how difficult a task that must have been. Thanks mom for taking such good care of us kids as we were growing up. We always had food in our bellies, clean clothes to wear, and a smile on our face. You were always there for us. You've given me strength, character, and taught me how to be a good parent of which I am most proud. Thanks also for the most precious gift a mother could give her child, the gift of love.

All my love, Rick

Preface

The Student-Athlete and College Recruiting is written for the millions of high school student-athletes all across the country. My intent is to assist all athletes aspiring to compete at the collegiate level. If you get only one thing out of this material, please make sure you understand the importance of **ACADEMICS!** After all, when the game is over and your college athletic career is complete, the diploma you hold in your hands will open the doors to your future and stay with you forever.

Good luck and God bless all of you, Rick Wire

Testimonials

"This book is a great tool for all athletes looking at Division 1, 2 or 3. It teaches you how to market yourself and also helps prepare you mentally and physically for college athletics. It is invaluable to not only the "Blue Chippers" but also the not-so-highly recruited athlete. If I had a tool like this to help me through the recruiting process, it would have been a tremendous asset.!"

Kyle Brady, NFL Veteran

"The information in this program has been invaluable to our student-athletes and coaches. I highly recommend it to all Athletic Directors, Counselors, Coaches, and parents."
Mick Morrison, Athletic Director, Cathedral City High School, Cathedral City, CA

"This book has become the universal tool for use by our coaching staff throughout the entire school district. As a coach, I have everything I need to help guide our student-athletes with very little cost to the family."
Christ Christenson, Counselor, Neenah High School, Neenah, WI

"This book enabled me to pass along valuable information to all our student-athletes, male and female, to help us confidently prepare them for college athletics."
Larry Moore, Athletic Director, Georgetown High School, Georgetown, TX

Rick Wire's insightful perspective and ambitious drive has led us to participate in our daughters recruiting process which has resulted in college coaches calling and emailing our daughter's varsity coach during her sophomore year. I would highly recommend purchasing Rick Wire's book along with booking an engagement for him to share all that he has learned and performed himself, over the years. You'll be glad you did.

Earl and Michelle, Sugar Land, Texas

Rick Wire's college recruiting seminar was AMAZING!! The information presented was extremely valuable to our students and parents. Dynamite Sports' website for coaches, counselors, students and parents is an INCREDIBLE resource for our entire community. I have been through the college recruiting process personally. Rick's presentation and the Dynamite Website should be titled - "Everything I Wish I Knew the First Time". These resources and book will save our community money in the recruiting process AND help them get more money in scholarships and grants.

Matt Shomper, Athletic Director, Tippecanoe High School, Ohio

What a great help your book was to me and my family. I have a few years grace until I get started with my youngest son who is a freshman at St. John's College here in DC.

Michael G. Leemhuis, M.A. Ed., CCM, PGA, Chief Operating Officer, Congressional Country Club Bethesda, Maryland 20817 USA

Rick Wire and Dynamite Sports have provided our athletic community with a tremendous online resource. Parents, teachers, coaches and athletes are provided a consistent message filled with accurate and up to date information. In Prince William County, we appreciate the time and expertise that Dynamite Sports has provided to enhance the opportunities for all of our student-athletes.

Fred Milbert – Supervisor of Health & Physical Education, Athletics, & ROTC, Prince William County Schools

The Farmington Athletic Department has provided our student-athletes, parents, and counselor and coaches this valuable recruiting tool for three years. With all of the information that athletic directors, principals, counselors, parents and student-athletes get thrown their way, this is the best resource that I have seen that sorts it all out and delivers the information in a very concise and user friendly way. I highly recommend it.

Denny Noe, Athletic Director, Farmington Public Schools

The "Guiding the College-Bound Athlete Seminar" is a powerful and realistic message that captivates the listener. You can sense the passion and overall concern for the student-athlete. The Student-Athlete & College Recruiting handbook is a must have for anyone ready to get started on this journey. Rick Wire & Dynamite Sports brings a dynamic and "light" approach to one of the most important decisions in a student-athlete's life. I host one of their seminars every two years!

Brian Weidler, Athletic Administrator, Palmyra Area High School, PA

Preface

PREFACE

Introduction

Welcome to *The Student-Athlete and College Recruiting*. Let me give you some background on how I created this educational tool. I had a son, Coy, that wanted to be a collegiate athlete. He worked hard both academically and athletically to put himself in a position to be recruited by major colleges. His hard work and dedication paid off. On July 1st, after his junior year, he accepted a full athletic scholarship to attend Stanford University.

The knowledge I gained during the recruiting process my son went through is invaluable. Over a four-year period I acquired a lot of information about recruiting. When my son was a freshman, I talked to parents of senior athletes to see what the recruiting process was like for them, what they liked, and disliked about it, and what they would do differently if they could do it all over again. I took all that information and formulated my own plan for creating the best possible recruiting experience for my son. I came to the following conclusion.

Basically there are three ways to go:

- You can start as early as your freshman year, taking two unofficial visits to colleges on your own and then committing early.

- You can go through the entire recruiting process taking all your official visits and committing on the day of signing.

- You can find a blend between these two and take a few official visits and then verbally commit before the signing date.

Evaluating Your Child's Talent

Most children grow up with dreams of being the next Michael Jordan, Florence Griffith-Joyner, Emmitt Smith, Monica Seles, or Mark McGwire. But in reality, less than 1/10th of 1% of high school athletes ever come close to reaching this level. Nevertheless, there is nothing wrong with having dreams. But when the time comes to choose a college and compete at the collegiate level, our children must be honest and realistic about their talent and abilities. We can't allow them to set the **CHIN BAR** so high that they could never reach it. An example would be a 5'2" basketball player that wants to go to North Carolina to play basketball; or, an offensive lineman that is 5' 8" - 210 lbs. that wants to play for Notre Dame; or even a female soccer player that runs a 7.3 - 40 yd. dash that wants to play for the University of Texas.

I believe that the first critical step our children take in considering college athletics is evaluating their own talent level and setting attainable goals. Use the following scenario as a barometer to measure your child's talent level.

If your child **STARTS AS A FRESHMAN** on the varsity squad there is a good chance they may have the talent to play at the NCAA Division I level. If they start for 2 or 3 years on the varsity, they are probably more suited for the NCAA Division II level. If they only start their senior year on varsity, NCAA Division III is probably the level where they should concentrate. There are exceptions to this philosophy, but they are **FEW** and **FAR** between. Some high school coaches prefer not to start freshman because of either maturity, reasons or maybe there is a senior at that same position that they feel has earned the right to play. And, a player that started as a freshman at a **SMALL SCHOOL** might not have been able to crack the line-up as a sophomore at a **BIGGER SCHOOL**.

Sit down with your high school coach and ask him/her to help evaluate your talent and what level of college athletics fits you best. They will have a valuable perspective in helping you evaluate your talent. It is **EXTREMELY** important to determine what level of college athletics your child is best suited for. If they choose the wrong level, they may not have a chance of getting a piece of that **ATHLETIC SCHOLARSHIP PIE**. Or worse, it could ruin their entire college experience. Remember, it's not your perception of your child's abilities and talent that gets the athletic scholarship. It's the perception of a college coach who may be hundreds or even thousands of miles away. Their opinion is the only one that **REALLY** counts.

ACADEMICS

Dealing with Academics

In order to be eligible to compete as a freshman in college, you need to make certain that you meet the academic eligibility requirements of the Athletic Association where you are planning to participate. Whether you hope to compete in the NCAA, NAIA, or the NJCAA, you must realize that it's not just athletic talent that determines whether you will be able to participate. Just as important, if not more, are the academic requirements that relate to the course schedule you carry each year in high school.

There are good reasons for these academic requirements. Most importantly, you need to be prepared for the rigorous academic schedule you will have in college. The best preparation for this is a solid foundation at the high school level. Remember, the odds of a high school football player making it to the pros are about 6,000 to 1. The odds for a high school basketball player are 10,000 to 1. What really matters in the long run is receiving a good college education.

Each athletic association has their own initial eligibility standards, which is determined using a combination of required Core Courses, a core grade point average, and a standardized test score. Qualifying or not qualifying to these standards will determine whether you can compete as a freshman. Meeting these standards **DOES NOT** necessarily mean that you will be accepted for admission into an institution, only that you will be eligible to compete as a freshman.

It's important to meet with your high school counselor early and develop a plan that will insure you will meet NCAA, NAIA and NJCAA eligibility requirements. Discuss which standardized test you should take. It's best to start early, maybe in your freshman year and include a few "weighted" courses in your schedule. This may give you an indication of where you are academically with respect to the scale of eligibility. Allow time to be involved in extra-curricular activities such as Key Club, Student Council, SADD, etc. Also, try to assume a leadership role in some of these activities. Colleges want a **WELL-ROUNDED** student-athlete.

Initial Eligibility Requirements

Athletes who want to compete at the NCAA Divisions I & II or the NAIA are required to pass Eligibility Standards. Those athletes who desire to compete at the NCAA Division III or Junior College level only need to be accepted into the college in order to compete as freshman. The section below provides detailed information regarding the requirements for each athletic association. Initial eligibility is achieved by successfully qualifying on the three major components: Core Courses, GPA, and either an SAT or ACT test score.

The NCAA Eligibility Requirements

The NCAA has established the following eligibility requirements which will affect all student-athletes who wish to compete at the Division I or II level. Parents, student-athletes and especially school officials working closely with students-athletes should be aware of the freshman-eligibility standards.

If a student-athlete plans to complete in college athletics as a freshman they must:

- Graduate from high school
- Division I & II requires that a student-athlete successfully complete a core curriculum of at least 16 academic courses.
- Division I requires that a student-athlete have a core GPA of 2.3 (based on a 4.0 scale) and a combined SAT score or a sum ACT score based on the Sliding Scale. Division II schools require a Core GPA of 2.2 (based on a 4.0 scale) for a full qualifier a Core GPA of 2.0 for a "Partial Qualifier". Both must also meet the corresponding SAT/ACT test scores on the qualifier index.
- Register with the NCAA Eligibility Center

After attaining Initial Eligibility, student-athletes enrolled in college must adhere to the following standards to maintain their eligibility:

- By the start of their 3rd year of college, complete 40% of their degree requirements
- By the start of their 4th year of college, complete 60% of their degree requirements
- By the start of their 5th year of college, complete 80% of their degree requirements.

Qualifier or Non-qualifier

NCAA Division I schools require all student-athletes to meet all of the above requirements. If a student-athlete fails to achieve all of these requirements they will be a **"Non-qualifier"**.

A non-qualifier is not eligible for regular season competition or practice during the first academic year in residence and then has three or four seasons of eligibility remaining depending on the completion of their degree requirements.

A non-qualifier may not receive athletics-related aid as a freshman, but may receive regular need-based financial aid if the school certifies that aid was granted without regard to athletics ability and is not from an athletic source.

NCAA Division II schools only require student-athletes to achieve a minimum of a 2.0 GPA in the 16 Core Courses and a minimum 820 SAT / 68 ACT test score and would then be a "Partial Qualifier."

A "partial qualifier" is eligible to practice with a team at its home facility and receive an athletic scholarship during his or her first year at a Division II school, and then has four seasons of competition remaining. But they may NOT play their freshman year.

To be classified a "partial qualifier" you're required to graduate from high school and meet one of the following requirements:

- Specified minimum SAT or ACT score

- Successful completion of a required core curriculum consisting of 16 core courses with a 2.000 core grade-point average.
- If a student-athlete fails to meet the requirements of a "Partial Qualifier" they would become a "Non-Qualifier."
- Non-qualifier: College-bound student-athletes may not practice, compete or receive athletics scholarships during their first year of enrollment at an NCAA Division II school.

The NAIA Eligibility Requirements

The NAIA recruitment process is less cumbersome, with fewer restrictions on the contact a student-athlete and coach may have. More frequent contact will assist in assuring that the student-athlete is comfortable with the choice of institution. In the event the student-athlete feels that the school or team is not the right fit, he/she can transfer to another NAIA institution and compete the next season without sitting out a year. We hope you strongly consider enrolling at an NAIA member institution.

There are many advantages to competing in NAIA sports. Besides the benefit of close-knit communities and smaller class sizes on the typical NAIA campus, NAIA athletics offer:

- Maximum opportunity to participate in regular season contests and National Championships.
- Flexibility to transfer without missing a season of eligibility.
- Fewer recruiting restrictions.
- Focus on the education and character development of the student-athlete.

The following criteria must be met in order for you to be eligible to represent a member institution in any manner:

YOU MUST, if an entering freshman, meet two of three entry level requirements.

1. Achieve a minimum of 18 on the Enhanced ACT or 860 on the SAT (Critical Reading and Math sections). Tests must be taken on a national testing date (residual tests are not acceptable). Scores must be achieved on a single test.
2. Achieve a minimum overall high school gpa of 2.0 on a 4.0 scale.
3. Graduate in the upper half of your high school graduating class.

More information regarding the NAIA organization may be obtained at www.naia.org or by telephone at 913.791.0044.

Core Course Requirements

Core Course requirements only apply at the NCAA D-I and D-II levels. Remember not all high school courses qualify as a core course. The High School guidance department submits a listing of courses to be considered as core courses. This listing is then evaluated by the NCAA to insure that all courses meet the following criteria:

A core course must be defined as a recognized academic course and qualify for high school graduation credit in one or a combination of the following areas: English, mathematics, natural/physical science, social science, foreign language, or non-doctrinal religion/philosophy;

NCAA Division I Core Course Requirements

(FULL QUALIFIER)

NCAA Division I institutions require prospective student-athletes successfully complete a core curriculum of at least 16 academic courses in the following areas:

- 4 years of English
- 3 years of mathematics (Algebra I or higher)
- 2 years of social science
- 2 years of natural or physical science (including at least one laboratory class)
- 1 additional course in English, math or one of the two sciences
- 4 additional academic courses (including any of the above and/or foreign language, philosophy, etc.)

    Ten of the 16 core courses must be completed before the seventh semester (senior year) of high school.

    • Seven of the 10 core courses must be in English, math or natural/physical science.

    • Earn a core-course GPA of at least 2.300.

    • Earn an SAT combined score or ACT sum score matching the core-course GPA on the Division I sliding scale (NCAA D-I FULL QUALIFIER INDEX).

    • Graduate high school.

(ACADEMIC REDSHIRT)

• Complete 16 core courses.

• Earn a core-course GPA of at least 2.000.

• Earn an SAT combined score or ACT sum score matching the core-course GPA on the Division I sliding scale

• Graduate high school.

NCAA Division II Core Course Requirements

(FULL QUALIFIER)

NCAA Division II institutions require prospective student-athletes successfully complete the following core courses:

- 3 years of English
- 2 years of mathematics (Algebra I or higher)
- 2 years of social science
- 2 years of natural or physical science (including at least one laboratory class)
- 3 additional course in English, math or one of the two sciences
- 4 Four additional years of English, math, natural or physical science, social
- science, foreign language, comparative religion or philosophy
  - Complete 16 core courses.
  - Earn a core-course GPA of at least 2.200.
  - Earn an SAT combined score or ACT sum score matching the core-course GPA on the Division II full qualifier sliding scale
  - Graduate high school.
                    (PARTIAL QUALIFIER)
  - Complete 16 core courses.
  - Earn a core-course GPA of at least 2.000.
  - Earn an SAT combined score or ACT sum score matching the core-course GPA on the Division II partial qualifier sliding scale.
  - Graduate high school.

Obtaining a Core Course Listing

Each high school has a list of the courses that have been approved by the NCAA as "Core Courses". This list can usually be obtained from the school guidance counselor or by accessing the Core Course Database at www.eligibilitycenter.org. The procedure below provides directions on obtaining a core course listing from the Eligibility Center website.

1. Using an internet browser access the site at www.eligibilitycenter.org.
2. Locate and click on the Resources Option at the top of the screen.
3. Click on the U.S. Students options in the Resource Notebook.
4. Click on the List of Approved Core Courses option. This will open a new window.
5. Locate and click on the List of Approved Core Course. This is located on the left side of the screen.
6. If you know your High School Code enter it in the box provided and jump to step 9. If you don't know the 6-digit school code you can search by school name or use the "LOOKUP CODE" button.
7. Scroll to the state that your school is in and click on the appropriate selection depending on the city in which the school is located.
8. Now scroll to the city and click on the number that is listed beside your school. This will automatically fill in the School Code box and close the

popup window.

9. Now click on the SUBMIT button. Your Core Course listing will be displayed. This page usually shows the location details and the grading scales of the selected school. Click on the continue button to display the listing.

10. Using your browser functions, print this page for your reference.

Core Course Frequently Asked Questions

Q: How are core courses determined?

The NCAA Eligibility Center lists only those courses that qualify as a core course after receiving information provided by your high school principal. All approved courses appear on the high school's list of approved core courses. You can view a list of approved core courses on the NCAA Eligibility Center Web site at www.eligibilitycenter.net. Click on "List of Approved Core Courses" from the General Information page.

Q: Do I have to successfully complete the core courses used to satisfy the core course GPA requirement?

Yes. Students entering a Division I or a Division II college as freshmen must have satisfactorily completed all courses used to satisfy core-curriculum requirements. Satisfactory completion is defined as a non-failing grade (i.e., a grade of "D" or above).

Q: Can courses taken in the eighth grade satisfy core-course requirements?

Yes, courses taken in eighth grade will satisfy the core course requirements if the course appears on the high school transcript with a grade, and if the course appears on the high school's list of approved core courses and the course counts towards high school graduation.

Q: Can college courses count toward core course requirements?

Yes, a college course may be used as a core course if it is accepted by your high school and if the course

- Would be accepted for any other student;
- Is placed on your high school transcript (D-I only)
- Any college transcripts should also be sent to the eligibility center, and
- Meets all other requirements for a core course.

Q: Can I count credit-by-exam courses in my core course requirements?

No. Courses completed through credit-by-exam may not be used to satisfy core-course requirements.

Q: Can I count independent-study and Internet courses in my core course requirements?

Yes, if the following four conditions are met:

- The course meets core course requirements
- The Student and the instructor have access to each other during the course so that the instructor can teach, evaluate and provide assistance to the student
- Appropriate academic authorities evaluate the student's work according to the high school's academic policies; and
- The course is acceptable for any student to take and is placed on the high school transcript.

Q: Are vocational courses acceptable?

No. Traditional vocational courses are not acceptable. These include courses such as typing, auto mechanics, driver education and health.

Q: May courses for students with disabilities count as core courses?

Yes. If you have a diagnosed disability, you may use courses designed for students with disabilities to meet NCAA core course requirements. These courses must appear on the high school's list of approved core courses for a student to receive NCAA credit for the course. These courses must be similar in content and scope as a regular core course offered in that academic area. Check with your high school counselor.

Q: What if I leave high school after my junior year to enter an early admissions program?

You may receive a waiver of the initial-eligibility requirements if you enter an early admissions program (open to students solely on the basis of outstanding academic performance and promise), provided that for the last four semesters in high school, you maintained a cumulative minimum grade-point average of 3.500 (based on a maximum of 4.000), ranked in the top 20 percent of your class and met all other requirements for graduation from high school, and for Division I, the only remaining deficiency is in the core course area of English (i.e., lacking one year of English).

Q: Is there a way for me to be immediately eligible in Division I if I didn't complete my core courses in the first eight semesters?

At Division I institutions, if you repeat an entire term or academic year of high school, you may use appropriate courses taken during that term or year to fulfill the core-course requirements. However, if the repeated term or year occurs after graduation, the core courses you use must be taken at the high school from which you graduated. If core courses are completed beyond the eighth semester, your initial full-time college enrollment cannot occur until the next academic year. It is permissible to substitute the grades earned in postgraduate high school work in place of grades attained before graduation, provided the above mentioned conditions are satisfied.

Q: What do I need to present if I am in a home-schooling program?

All prospective student-athletes who are home-schooled will need to have their core course requirements analyzed by the NCAA Initial-Eligibility Waiver Committee. Please contact membership services for information regarding home-schooling.

Q: Can studies in a foreign country help satisfy core course requirements?

If you attended a secondary school outside the United States for all or a portion of your ninth through twelfth grades, different evaluation procedure must be applied to your international education documents. Write the eligibility center to request additional application forms or information concerning evaluation of international credentials. Remember, all students with coursework completed outside the United States must have original language documents and certified translations submitted for examination by the eligibility center.

Monitoring NCAA Eligibility Status

The form on page 16 may be used to assist you in keeping track of courses needed for athletic eligibility in NCAA colleges. Following the completion of each semester, fill out the areas on the form by checking off those requirements that have been met and marking the grade earned and date completed. Keep in mind that the checklist reflects the minimum requirements set forth by the NCAA. However, the requirements for admission into a particular college often times include more courses.

Step 1 Obtain Needed Documents

Obtain your high school's List of NCAA-Approved Core Courses, your report cards and current schedule.

Step 2 List Courses, Grades and Credits

Using the above document, fill in the course title, amount of credit earned and grade in the spaces provided. Only include courses on the high school's list of approved core courses.

Trimester courses receive .33 credit, semester courses receive .5 credit and year courses receive 1 full credit.

Step 3 Do the Math

Multiply the point value for the grade by the amount of credit earned to determine the quality points. Use the following grading scale unless your high school has a different scale on file with the Eligibility Center:

A - 4 points   B - 3 points   C - 2 points   D - 1 point

Note: The Eligibility Center does not use plus or minus grades when calculating your core course grade-point average. For example, grades of "B+" "B" and "B-" will be calculated as "B" and each will earn 3 quality points.

Step 4 Finalize Your GPA Calculation

To calculate your estimated core-course grade-point average, simply divide the total number of quality points for all core courses by the total number of core course units completed.

If you have 45 quality point and 13 core courses, divide 45 by 13 to get a 3.624 core GPA.

Note: This is for your personal use. The Eligibility Center will calculate your actual core course grade-point average once it has received your final transcript(s).

Step 5 Compare

To monitor your current eligibility status, use the appropriate standards for Division I or II to determine if you are projected to meet the NCAA initial eligibility requirements for grade-point average and core course units.

Note: In the event you complete more than the required core course units, the Eligibility Center will select the highest grades that satisfy the initial eligibility requirements to calculate your core course grade-point average.

GPA Requirements

The second component in Initial Eligibility is your Grade Point Average (GPA). Both the NCAA and the NAIA require a minimum GPA. Be aware that the NCAA GPA requirement is calculated using only the Core Courses. Along with the number of Core Courses in the requirement, D-I and D-II schools have different Core GPA requirements that students must meet in order to be eligible to play college sports during their freshman year.

NCAA D-I FULL QUALIFIER INDEX

CORE GPA	SAT	ACT	CORE GPA	SAT	ACT
3.550	400	37	2.750	810	59
3.525	410	38	2.725	820	60
3.500	430	39	2.700	830	61
3.475	440	40	2.675	840	61
3.450	460	41	2.650	850	62
3.425	470	41	2.625	860	63
3.400	490	42	2.600	860	64
3.375	500	42	2.575	870	65
3.350	520	43	2.550	880	66
3.325	530	44	2.525	890	67
3.300	550	44	2.500	900	68
3.275	560	45	2.475	910	69
3.250	580	46	2.450	920	70
3.225	590	46	2.425	930	70
3.200	600	47	2.400	940	71
3.175	620	47	2.375	950	72
3.150	630	48	2.350	960	73
3.125	650	49	2.325	970	74
3.100	660	49	2.300	980	75
3.075	680	50	2.299	990	76
3.050	690	50	2.275	990	76
3.025	710	51	2.250	1000	77
3.000	720	52	2.225	1010	78
2.975	730	52	2.200	1020	79
2.950	740	53	2.175	1030	80
2.925	750	53	2.150	1040	81
2.900	750	54	2.125	1050	82
2.875	760	55	2.100	1060	83
2.850	770	56	2.075	1070	84
2.825	780	56	2.050	1080	85
2.800	790	57	2.025	1090	86
2.775	800	58	2.000	1100	86

ACADEMIC REDSHIRT

17

NCAA D-II Schools

NCAA D-II schools require all **S/A**s to meet a minimum GPA & Test Score. If the **S/A** fails to achieve a qualifying Test Score or GPA, he may be classified as a **"Partial Qualifier."**

A "partial qualifier" is eligible to practice with a team at its home facility and receive an athletic scholarship during his first year at a D-II school. He then has four seasons of competition remaining.

A student who has not met the requirements for a "qualifier," but has graduated from high school and meets at least one of the following requirements will be classified a "partial qualifier:"

- Specified minimum SAT or ACT score

- Successful completion of a required core curriculum consisting of 16 core courses with a 2.000 core grade point average

A "nonqualifier" is a student who has not graduated from high school or who has presented neither the core curriculum grade point average, nor an SAT/ACT score required for a qualifier. A "nonqualifier" is not eligible for regular season competition and practice during the first academic year in residence and then has four seasons of competition.

A "nonqualifier" may not receive athletic-related aid as a freshman, but may receive regular need-based financial aid with the school's certification that the aid was granted without regard to athleticsability.

Test Scores If a student plans to attend an NCAA Division II college or university in the 2019-20 or 2020-21 academic years, use the following charts to understand the core-course GPA they will need to meet NCAA Division II requirements. A combined SAT score is calculated by adding critical reading and math subscores. An ACT sum score is calculated by adding English, math, reading and science subscores. A student may take the SAT or ACT an unlimited number of times before he or she enrolls full time in college. If a student takes either test more than once, the best subscores from each test are used for the academic certification process.

DIVISION II
FULL QUALIFIER SLIDING SCALE

CORE GPA	SAT	ACT	CORE GPA	SAT	ACT
3.300 & above	400	37	2.425	840	61
3.275	410	38	2.400	850	62
3.250	430	39	2.375	860	63
3.225	440	40	2.350	860	64
3.200	460	41	2.325	870	65
3.175	470	41	2.300	880	66
3.150	490	42	2.275	890	67
3.125	500	42	2.250	900	68
3.100	520	43	2.225	910	69
3.075	530	44	2.200	920	70 & above
3.050	550	44			
3.025	560	45			
3.000	580	46			
2.975	590	46			
2.950	600	47			
2.925	620	47			
2.900	630	48			
2.875	650	49			
2.850	660	49			
2.825	680	50			
2.800	690	50			
2.775	710	51			
2.750	720	52			
2.725	730	52			
2.700	740	53			
2.675	750	53			
2.650	750	54			
2.625	760	55			
2.600	770	56			
2.575	780	56			
2.550	790	57			
2.525	800	58			
2.500	810	59			
2.475	820	60			
2.450	830	61			

DIVISION II
PARTIAL QUALIFIER SLIDING SCALE

CORE GPA	SAT	ACT	CORE GPA	SAT	ACT
3.050 & above	400	37	2.175	840	61
3.025	410	38	2.150	850	62
3.000	430	39	2.125	860	63
2.975	440	40	2.100	860	64
2.950	460	41	2.075	870	65
2.925	470	41	2.050	880	66
2.900	490	42	2.025	890	67
2.875	500	42	2.000	900	68
2.850	520	43			& above
2.825	530	44			
2.800	550	44			
2.775	560	45			
2.750	580	46			
2.725	590	46			
2.700	600	47			
2.675	620	47			
2.650	630	48			
2.625	650	49			
2.600	660	49			
2.575	680	50			
2.550	690	50			
2.525	710	51			
2.500	720	52			
2.475	730	52			
2.450	740	53			
2.425	750	53			
2.400	750	54			
2.375	760	55			
2.350	770	56			
2.325	780	56			
2.300	790	57			
2.275	800	58			
2.250	810	59			
2.225	820	60			
2.200	830	61			

NCAA CORE COURSE WORKSHEET

Note: This worksheet is provided to assist you in monitoring your progress toward meeting NCAA Initial eligibility standards. The Eligibility Center will determine your official status after graduation

English 3 (D-II) or 4 (D-I) years required			
Course Title	Credit	Grade	Quality
Total English Units			
Mathematics 2 (D-II) or 3 (D-I) years required			
Course Title	Credit	Grade	Quality
Total Mathematical Units			
Natural / Physical Science 2 years required			
Course Title	Credit	Grade	Quality
Total Natural / Physical Science Units			
Additional Year of English, Math, Natural / Physical Science 1 (D-I) or 3 (D-II)			
Course Title	Credit	Grade	Quality
Total Additional Units			
Social Sciences 2 years required			
Course Title	Credit	Grade	Quality
Total Social Sciences Units			
Additional Academic Courses 4 years required			
Course Title	Credit	Grade	Quality
Total Electives Units			
Core Course GPA			
Total Quality Points	**Total # of Credits**		**# of Core Courses**

SLIDING SCALE OF ELIGIBILITY

NCAA Division I uses a Sliding Scale to determine whether a student-athlete satisfies the GPA requirement. The Sliding Scale consists of a Core GPA and a Standardized Test Score (SAT, ACT). Based on either component there is a matching component that must be achieved. Refer to the following tables

Standardized Testing Options

The third component of Initial Eligibility is the Standardized Test. There are currently two standardized tests which are made available to college-bound students; they are the SAT I and the ACT. These tests are used as part of the admissions requirement into college. All colleges require an applicant to submit a standardized test score in order to measure a student's ability to do college-level work.

Because courses and grading standards vary widely from school to school, scores on standardized tests, like the SAT I and the ACT, help colleges compare your academic achievements with those of students from different schools.

The following sections provide helpful information regarding the PSAT / SAT I and the PLAN / ACT tests.

The PSAT Test

The PSAT stands for preliminary SAT. It's a standardized test that provides first hand practice for the SAT Reasoning Test. It also gives you a chance to enter the National Merit Scholarship programs.

The PSAT measures:

- Critical reading
- Math problem solving skills
- Writing skills

The PSAT is a junior-level test, although many students benefit by taking it earlier, typically in their sophomore year. Sophomores will be provided with a sophomore percentile so that they can compare their performance to other sophomores who are also planning on going to college.

You must sign up for the test at your high school or one in your community. High schools usually administer the PSAT in October. There is a fee for the PSAT, and College Board makes fee waivers available to schools for juniors from low-income families who can't afford the test fee. See your counselor for more information about fee waivers.

The SAT Tests

The SAT is a three-hour and forty-five minute test that measures students' skills in critical reading, mathematic reasoning, and writing. Many colleges and universities use the SAT as one indicator among others-class rank, high school GPA, extracurricular activities, personal essay, and teacher recommendations of a student's readiness to do college-level work. SAT scores are compared with the scores of other applicants, and the accepted scores at an institution, and can be used as a basis for awarding merit-based financial aid.

All of the sections are scored on a scale of 200-800; highest possible combined score is 2400. Students may take the SAT as often as they like, but all scores except those taken before high school are sent to colleges. The NCAA Eligibility Center will only use the scores achieved on the critical reading and mathematic reasoning sections to pass the Qualifier Index. There is a basic fee for the SAT test which is administered several times a year. Fee waivers are available to schools for students from low-income families who can't afford the test fee. Consult the link provided below for the current testing dates.

www.thestudentathleteandcollegerecruiting.com/testing_dates

The SAT subject tests are one-hour, multiple-choice, subject specific test. They measure how much students know about a particular academic subject and how well they can apply that knowledge. There are 22 specific Subject Tests that cover english, history, social studies, mathematics, science and languages.

You may obtain additional information and also register to take tests at the College Board website. The URL is www.collegeboard.org.

SAT Frequently Asked Questions

Q: What does the SAT cost? What about fee waivers?

The fee for the SAT Test varies, you can check the current fee at www.collegeboards.org. Students who cannot afford test fees can apply for fee waivers to cover test fees. Fee waivers are not permitted with late registrations.

Q: What do SAT scores look like?

The SAT has three scores, each on the scale of 200-800. Your score will include writing (W 200-800), mathematics (M 200-800), and critical reading (CR 200-800).

Q: What are the similarities and differences between the SAT and the PSAT?

Both the SAT, and the PSAT/NMSQT measure reasoning skills in critical reading, writing, and mathematics. The PSAT/NMSQT contains actual SAT questions, but it is designed to be slightly easier than the SAT. The PSAT/NMSQT is 2 hours and 10 minutes, whereas the SAT takes 3 hours and 45 minutes. The SAT is used for college admissions, but PSAT/NMSQT scores are not sent to colleges. The PSAT/NMSQT Score Report gives you personalized feedback on areas in which you could improve. Taking the PSAT/NMSQT gives you a chance to qualify for scholarship and recognition programs and is the best practice for the SAT.

Q: Are some SAT tests more difficult than other ones?

All editions of the SAT are developed using the same test specifications. Even if there are tiny differences in difficulty from test to test, a statistical process called "equating" ensures that a score for a test taken on one date or at one place is equivalent to a score for a test taken on another date or in another place. The rumors that the SAT in one month, say in October, is easier, are false.

Q: Are all SAT questions multiple-choice?

In addition to multiple-choice questions, the SAT has a 25-minute written essay and 10 student-produced response math questions. The math questions ask you to fill in, or "grid-in," your own answers using a special section of the answer sheet.

Q: What's the difference between the SAT and Subject Tests?

The SAT measures what you have learned in school and how well you can apply that knowledge. It assesses how well you analyze and solve problems. SAT scores are used for college admissions purposes because the test predicts college success. The SAT Subject Tests are one-hour, primarily multiple-choice tests in specific subjects. Subject Tests measure knowledge or skills in a particular subject and your ability to apply that knowledge.

Q: How many times can you take the test?

You can take the test as many times as you want. Your official score report shows your current test score, in addition to scores for up to six SAT and six Subject Test administrations.

Q: Which test should I take?

Most colleges require the SAT for admission and many other schools require both the SAT and Subject Tests for admissions purposes or placement. Additionally, some colleges require specific Subject Tests while others allow you to choose which tests you take. It's best to check directly with the college admissions offices.

Q: Should I take the SAT first or the Subject Tests first?

Most students take the SAT in the spring of their junior year and again in the fall of their senior year of high school. Because Subject Tests are directly related to course work, it's helpful to take tests such as World History, Biology E/M, Chemistry, or Physics as soon as possible after completing the course in the subject, even as a freshman or sophomore, while the material is still fresh in your mind. You'll do better on other tests like languages after at least two years of study.

Q: What will I be asked to write about in the essay?

The essay question will ask you to develop a point of view on an issue and support it with examples from your studies and experience. You can answer the question successfully in many different ways. You won't have to have any prior knowledge about the topic to write an effective essay. However, you will have to answer the essay assignment directly.

Q: Will colleges see my essay?

A college will be able to view and print your essay only if you send that college your test scores. Writing scores may be used for admissions decisions and possibly for placement in English Composition courses.

Q: What do my SAT I scores tell college admission staff about me?

Your SAT scores can tell admissions staff members how well prepared you are for college-level academics.

Remember, that the SAT is only one of a number of factors that colleges consider when making admissions decisions. Other factors, such as your high school record, essays, recommendations, interviews, and extracurricular activities, also play a role in admissions decisions.

Q: Can the SAT I really show how well I'll do in my first year of college?

No single piece of information can predict with 100 percent certainty what your college grades will be. This is because many factors—including personal motivation—influence your college grades. Combined with your high school grades, the SAT is the best predictor of your success in college. The SAT, therefore, can be of great value to admissions officers and can help you find the right college match.

College admissions officers use SAT scores to help estimate how well students are likely to do at a particular college. For example, a college looks at the SAT scores, high school grade point average (GPA), and college grades of its freshman class. A college may find that students who scored between 450 and 550 on the SAT and maintained a B average in high school are the students who perform well at that school. Knowing your SAT scores and high school GPA helps the admissions officers make a decision about how likely it is that you'll succeed at that particular institution.

Q: What about students with disabilities?

Students with disabilities, whose documentation has been validated by the College Board, will receive testing accommodations. Students with disabilities that necessitate the use of a computer for writing will be able to do so for the essay portion of the writing section. Students with disabilities may request extended time for taking the SAT.

Q: Will taking a test preparation course help me?

It's hard to say. Test preparation courses run the gamut from inexpensive to pricey. The content they cover differs as well. You need to make the choice that fits best for you. Here's some factual information about short- and long-term programs to help you make your decision:

- Short-term programs (about 20 hours) improve scores an average of about 10 points on verbal and about 15 points on math.
- Longer programs (40 hours or so) improve scores an average of 15 to 20 points on verbal and 20 to 30 points on math.
- Math scores seem to benefit more from coaching than verbal scores do.
- Longer programs yield somewhat larger gains; however, beyond the first 20 or 30 hours of coaching, score gains are very minor.

Q: How do I send scores to colleges?

When you register for the SAT, you get four score reports included in the test fee. One of these should be 9999 (the NCAA Eligibility Center). If you need more than four an additional fee is required.

Q: I have just registered with the Eligibility Center and am not planning on taking the SAT again. How do I get my scores sent to the Eligibility Center?

If you need to have past scores sent to the Eligibility Center you can request a report to be sent by using the Score Sender service and pay the additional fee.

The PLAN

As a "Pre-ACT" test, the **PLAN** test is a powerful predictor of success on the ACT Assessment. The PLAN is administered in tenth grade and consists of four achievement tests covering English, Mathematics, Reading and Science. Use the PLAN to determine where you need to improve prior to taking the ACT. Check with your guidance counselor or the ACT website to determine when the PLAN is offered in your area.

The ACT

The ACT Assessment is a national college admission examination that is accepted by virtually all U.S. colleges and universities. This assessment consists of tests in:

- English
- Mathematics
- Reading
- Science

The ACT includes 215 multiple-choice questions and takes approximately 3 hours and 30 minutes to complete with breaks. Actual testing time is 2 hours and 55 minutes.

Each of the subject tests is scored on a scale of 1-36. Totaling the scores of each section will give you the composite score. Dividing the composite score by 4 will give you the average test score.

ACT added a 30-minute Writing Test as an optional component to the ACT Assessment. Students should check with the institution they are applying to regarding their writing test requirement.

You may take the ACT Assessment as often as you wish. Many students take the test twice, once as a junior and again as a senior. Unlike the SAT if you take the test more than once, you control what scores are sent to colleges or scholarship programs.

In the U.S., the ACT is administered on five national test dates, in October, December, February, April, and June. In selected states, the ACT is also offered in late September. The basic registration fee includes reporting scores to up to four college choices, but you must provide valid college codes at time of registration. Fee waivers are available to schools for Juniors from low-income families who can't afford the test fee. Consult http://www.thestudentathleteandcollegerecruiting.com/testing_dates for current testing dates. You can register or find additional information at www.act.org

ACT Frequently Asked Questions

Q: Can students with disabilities take the ACT?

Yes. ACT is committed to serving students with disabilities by providing reasonable accommodations appropriate to the student's disability.

Q: Is non-Saturday testing available?

Yes, Non-Saturday testing is available only in remote areas or for students who cannot test on Saturday because of religious convictions.

Q: When should I test?

First, check the application deadlines of all the colleges and scholarship agencies to which you might want to apply. Pick a test date that is at least two months prior to these deadlines. It typically takes four to eight weeks after a test date to receive your score report.

Q: What if I can't afford the registration fee?

If you can't afford the registration fee, you may be eligible for a fee waiver from ACT. Funds are limited, and once they have been exhausted, requests for waivers will be denied. If you are eligible, you may use up to two fee waivers total. The waiver has been used once you register, even if you do not test on the requested test date.

To be eligible, you must meet the following requirements:

1. You currently attend high school as a junior or senior.
2. You meet at least one indicator of economic need listed on the ACT fee waiver form.

Q: Is the ACT offered in languages other than English?

No, the ACT Assessment is offered only in English.

Q: Is extended time allowed for examinees whose native language is not English?

Extended-time testing is available only for students with diagnosed disabilities and is not available solely on the basis of limited English proficiency.

Q: What materials are available to help me prepare?

Check out the following ACT materials available at www.act.org.

- Preparing for the ACT — A free booklet available through most high schools and colleges which includes valuable information about the test and a complete practice test with scoring key. This booklet is also downloadable at the ACT website in PDF format.
- ACT Online Prep — The ACT test prep program created by ACT test developers in now online
- The Real ACT Prep Guide — This is the official prep book from the creators of the ACT. This is the only guide to include three real tests, each with an optional Writing Test.

The NCAA Eligibility Center

The NCAA Eligibility Center certifies that college-bound athletes who wish to compete in Division I or II athletic programs have met necessary academic requirements and are of amateur status. NCAA colleges and universities set these regulations to ensure all student-athletes meet NCAA standards, including required core courses.

Certification

When you register with the Eligibility Center and provide basic information regarding your address, high school, year of graduation etc., the center will begin the process of certifying your academic status. This certification will be based on standardized test scores, your grade-point average and the core courses that you take while in high school.

In addition, you will be asked to provide answers to several questions relative to your athletic participation and any agreements you may have with an agent or professional team. Based on the information you provide, the eligibility center will determine if you are still an amateur, or if you have violated NCAA amateurism rules.

Registration Process

To register with the Eligibility Center, you must create an account at www.eligibilitycenter.org. After you create your account you will be asked to complete the forms in the following sections

- About Me – This section contains personal information, your name, address, birth date, etc.
- Coursework – Here you need to provide information regarding the schools that you attended for grades 9 through 12. If you have attended more than one school, you will need to provide that information as well. (Note: an official transcript will need to be sent from any additional schools that you attended.)
- Sport – In this section, you will select the sport(s) that you plan to participate in at the college level. They will also request information for any high school, club team that you participated with, and events that you attended during your high school career.
- Payment – Here they will need your payment information. You can use a credit or debit card, e-check, or fee waiver.

Fee Waivers

If a U.S. student-athlete has already received a fee waiver (not state voucher) for the ACT or SAT, then they are also eligible for a fee waiver from the NCAA Eligibility Center. A high school official must submit your fee waiver documentation online.

NCAA Eligibility Center Frequently Asked Questions

Q: Do I have to register with the eligibility center?

Yes. If you want to participate in Division I or II athletics as a freshman, you must register and be certified academically and as an amateur by the eligibility center. Note that certification from the eligibility center pertains only to whether you meet the NCAA requirements for participation as a freshman in Division I or II and has no bearing on your admission to a particular institution.

Q: How do I register?

The only method is to register online. Go to the NCAA Eligibility Center website. Select prospective students-athlete and then register as a U.S or international student. Complete the online registration and include your credit or debit card information for the registration fee. (The fee can be waived if you received a waiver of the ACT or SAT fee.)

Q: When is the best time for me to register?

Register at the beginning of your junior year in high school. If you do not submit all required documents, your file will be incomplete and will be discarded after three years. After that time, you will need to re-register and pay your fee again.

Q: Is there a deadline to register?

No. However, you must be certified as a qualifier before you can receive an athletic scholarship or practice or compete at a Division I or II college during your first year of enrollment.

Q: What if I plan on attending a Division III or a junior college. Should I still register?

Division III and junior colleges do not require the eligibility center to approve initial eligibility. Although by registering you will be prepared should a Division II college offer you athletic aid or should you plan to transfer and need amateurism certification.

Q: What if I was home schooled for all or part of high school?

Students who were home schooled for any part of high school (grades nine through 12) must now register with the NCAA Eligibility Center. The Eligibility Center will process all home-school certifications. There will no longer be the need for institutions to file initial-eligibility waivers for students who have been home schooled.

Q: What if I have attended more than one high school?

If you have attended multiple high schools since ninth grade, the eligibility center must receive an official transcript for each school. Transcripts can come directly from each school or from the high school from which you are graduating. Check with your high school counselor.

Q: Are standardized test scores required?

Yes, qualifying test scores are required for participation at both Division I and Division II colleges. If you intend to participate at either a Division I or II school, the test scores must be sent to the eligibility center directly from the testing agency. If you are registered with the eligibility center, you can mark code 9999 as a selected institution to receive your scores.

Q: How does a home-schooled student register with the Eligibility Center? What documents are required?

Home-schooled students should register with the Eligibility Center by visiting the Eligibility Center Web site at www.eligibilitycenter.org. Create an account and follow the prompts.

After registering, the home-schooled student must provide the following information to the Eligibility Center:

- Standardized test score (must be sent directly from the testing agency);
- Transcript (home school transcript and any other transcript from other high schools, community colleges, etc.);
- Proof of high-school graduation;
- Evidence that home schooling was conducted in accordance with state law:
- Lists of texts used throughout home schooling (text titles, publisher, in which courses texts were used).

Q: What will the Eligibility Center provide to the colleges that are recruiting me?

The eligibility center will send your eligibility and amateur status to any Division I or II college that requests it. Please note that the eligibility center will not send your information at your request; rather, the college must make the request for that information. Additionally, if no member institution requests your eligibility status, a final certification decision may not be processed.

Q: What are the disadvantages of not registering with the Eligibility Center?

Before an official visit can be taken to a Division I school they must have on campus an official transcript and a standardized test score. Division II schools only need a test score. These items are provided to the institutions through the eligibility center. If the eligibility center does not have your documents, then the high school has to provide them before your visit or it will be canceled.

Q: I am planning on transferring to a Division I or II institution from a junior college. All I need is my Amateur certification; do I have to receive an academic and an amateur certification?

You will definitely need to receive an amateurism certification. However, you may not need an academic certification. The institution that is recruiting you will be able to advise you on this matter based on your specific academic record. You will still need to pay the flat fee for registration even if you only need the amateur certification.

Suggested Academic Time Line

The information below reflects a recommended course load in order to complete the core course requirements. The NCAA does not require that these classes be taken in specific years of high school, only that they are taken before graduation. Remember, you are not only trying to succeed as an athlete at the collegiate level, but also as a student. Thus, it is important that you not limit yourself to only meeting the **MINIMUM** requirements outlined previously. It is far more beneficial for you to exceed these requirements and to schedule the most challenging courses (ie Honors, AP courses) you are able to handle. This will help ensure your success as a student-athlete at the college level.

Grade 9

- Follow the suggested academic core courses. Remember, this is the minimum required by the NCAA. Be certain to take the most challenging courses you are able to handle throughout high school.
- Also, work up to your best potential on the athletic field. Build a strong foundation to carry you through your high school career.

Grade 10

- Continue to progress towards completion of the academic courses required by the NCAA. Keep working to your best potential.
- Take the PSAT in October of this academic year. It is only offered once per year. Evaluate your scores and seek help on your weak areas.
- Start researching various careers which translate into majors/courses of study for college. You may want to take interest, abilities, and/or values inventories to help you in your explorations. Match these career interests with courses in high school. If you are uncertain about your future career path, take a general college-prep curriculum. See your guidance counselor for assistance.
- Obtain a social security number if you do not already have one. Colleges require this on their applications.

Grade 11

- Continue with your best performance in your course work. Make sure you are meeting (and exceeding) NCAA requirements.
- Register early with the NCAA Eligibility Center. Remember, this must be done if you wish to play at a Division I or II college.
- Take the SAT/ACT in fall or winter of this academic year. Compare your grade point average with these test scores and the qualifier index. Retake the SAT/ACT in the spring if scores are not where they need to be. Take any SAT II (specific subject tests) required by the colleges to which you wish to apply.
- Begin searching for schools that meet your needs – academic standards, majors of study, athletic teams, social events, etc. Involve your parents, guidance counselor, coaches, and significant others in this process.
- Make unofficial visits to the schools you are interested in attending.
- After your junior year, check you NCAA Eligibility Status to insure that your transcript and test scores were received. If you have attended any other high schools, make sure a transcript is sent to the eligibility center from each high school.

Grade 12

- Ensure that all academic course work required by the NCAA and college admissions will be met by the end of the year. Avoid "senioritis" and concentrate on taking challenging courses and keeping your grades up.

- Take a fall **SAT/ACT**, if needed. Also, take any advanced placement tests for which you qualify.

- Make **official visits** to schools. Visit any additional colleges you are interested in attending.

- Complete your **college applications and financial aid forms** well before the deadline date. If teacher recommendations are needed, allow plenty of time for teachers to complete their forms.

- Once you have received notice from the schools regarding your acceptance/ scholarship status, weigh all your options. Evaluate these options with your family and inform all of the colleges involved of your final decision.

International Student-Athletes

The recruitment of international prospective student-athletes (S-A's) is significantly more challenging than the recruitment of domestic prospective student-athletes. The purpose of this section is to outline the steps involved in the recruitment of a foreign S-A – please consult the Compliance Office frequently throughout recruitment to ensure that the process goes as smoothly as possible.

Freshman or Transfer S-A?

This is a key first step. A student-athlete is an entering freshman if he/she has graduated from secondary school (high school) and has not entered a university or post-secondary school as a full-time student. By contrast, S-A's will be considered a four-year college transfer if he/she is or was enrolled as a regular full-time student in any foreign university or other post-secondary school. The Office of Admissions will make the determination between enrollments in secondary vs. post-secondary schooling and between full-time and part-time enrollment.

Freshmen – NCAA Eligibility Center

All incoming freshmen S-A's must be certified by the NCAA Eligibility Center. Foreign S-A's must have their secondary school submit transcripts (with official translations) and standardized test scores (directly from the testing agency) to the NCAA Eligibility Center (via mail, not fax) for certification. Foreign S-A's must meet applicable secondary school core-curriculum and grade point average requirements as set forth in the "NCAA Guide to International Academic Standards" and must also present a corresponding standardized test score. Foreign S-A's must register with the Eligibility Center and pay the registration fee.

The Eligibility Center has a special registration and information form for foreign S-A's – this form can be obtained at www.eligibilitycenter.org or via the Compliance Office. Please note that the Eligibility Center certification often takes substantially longer for international prospects than for domestic prospects. For more information about the Eligibility Center process for international prospective student-athletes, please see the following information.

Recruiting Checklist - Freshman
- Review S-A's historical background with Compliance Office
- Register with the NCAA Eligibility Center, pay the registration fee, and complete Eligibility Center application for international students
- Submit all original secondary school transcripts (with English translation) directly from S-A's educational institution to Eligibility Center and Admissions Office
- Submit SAT or ACT scores directly from testing agency to Eligibility Center and Admissions Office
- Submit TOEFL scores directly from testing agency to Admissions Office

Recruiting Checklist - Transfers
- Review S-A's historical background with Compliance Office
- Have Admissions Office review unofficial copy of S-A's college transcripts to ensure that S-A meets all transfer rules
- If attempting to meet Conference transfer exception based on one year of college attendance, register with Eligibility Center, submit secondary school transcript, and request certification without test score.
- Have Admissions Office contact S-A's collegiate institution(s) in order to verify the S-A's semesters of full-time enrollment and to ensure eligibility for the Non-sponsored Sport Exception
- Complete admissions application for international students and pay application fee.
- Submit TOEFL scores directly from testing agency to Admissions Office

Participation after 21st Birthday

Any participation in organized sports competition by a prospective S-A during each 12-month period after the S-A's 21st birthday and prior to initial full-time enrollment in any post-secondary institution shall count as one season of Division I competition in that sport. For example, if a student turns 21 in January, participates in organized sports competition that spring (including national teams, tournaments, leagues, etc.), and then commences full-time enrollment in August, the student would be charged with one season of Division I competition. Note that it is possible for an individual to be charged with two seasons of competition during the same calendar year. For example, a student-athlete that turns 21 in October, competes in November, enrolls full-time in January, and competes for a university in February would use two seasons of competition – one under the 21st birthday legislation and one for representing the university in intercollegiate competition.

Admissions

All prospective student-athletes must satisfy the admissions policy in accordance with the university's regular admissions procedures. Foreign prospects may be required to complete an International Student Application and pay an application fee as well as any applicable late fees. School transcripts in the original language and English translations must be sent to the institutions Office of Admissions.

TOEFL (Test of English as a Foreign Language)

In order to be admitted all international S-A's must achieve a 500 on the written TOEFL examination or a 61 on the computer-based version. Incoming S-A's that are unable to achieve the necessary TOEFL score may be eligible for conditional admittance. More information regarding the TOEFL is available at http://www.toefl.com.

Related Internet Sites

General College Information

American Universities . . . . www.clas.ufl.edu/au
College Board Online (SAT) . . . . .www.collegeboard.org
ACT, Inc. . . . . .www.actstudent.org
Peterson's College Search . . . . www.petersons.com
The Princeton Review . . . . www.review.com
Colleges and Universities . . . . http://education.yahoo.com/

College Application Sites

CollegeLink . . . . .www.collegelink.com

Financial Aid and Scholarship Sites

FinAid: Financial Aid Information . . . . .www.finaid.org
FAFSA . . . . https://studentaid.ed.gov/sa/fafsa
College Net . . . . www.collegenet.com
Expan. . . . . .www.collegeboard.org

Career Information Sites

College Board Careers . . . . . . www.collegeboard.org/career/bin/career.pl
Career Resource Center . . . . www.careers.org

ATHLETICS

Most student-athletes don't realize the commitment, sacrifice and discipline it takes to play at the collegiate level. There are physical and mental demands you will need to overcome. When college athletes are asked, "What is the biggest difference between college and high school athletics", the three most common answers given were:

- The competition level is so much higher.
- The workout routine is very regimented.
- Time management is very difficult.

The following sections will point out how to handle not only the mental and physical aspects of collegiate athletics, but also give you guidelines on the type of athlete colleges are looking for, and how to set goals to achieve your dreams.

Athletics Strength Training

If you're really serious about being a college athlete, you have to develop a strength and conditioning program right now. **COMPETING** is the key word. If you're afraid of hard work, dedication, and putting forth that extra effort then close your eyes, relax, and have a nice day! Now if you're **HUNGRY**, ready to step in and make a contribution, **PAY ATTENTION!** Complete muscular development, for both male and female athletes, must be stressed at the high school level.

Let's start with the 3 core lifts. Although I believe the **BENCH PRESS** is an important exercise and is used to generate overall strength conditioning, it is highly overrated. Many athletes make the mistake of over emphasizing the bench press and neglecting other areas. Never place too much emphasis on an exercise that is done on your back. You've probably heard someone say, "So and so can bench press 500 pounds," and that's great, but if he does, chances are he also does squats, power cleans, and supplements the major muscle groups with other exercises. All that power and strength mean nothing if you can't put it into motion and maintain the intensity for one hour, nine (9) innings, five (5) sets, four (4) quarters, or three (3) periods!

If I had to pick one exercise that would benefit every sport, it would be the POWER CLEAN. Because of the complexity and difficulty in performing this movement correctly, it isn't well liked! I've also found that the exercises you "LEAST LIKE" are usually the area you need the most work. There is a misconception that power cleans cause undue stress on the back. Consequently, some coaches are hesitant to incorporate it into their training regimen. Sometimes it takes weeks, even months, to perform this lift correctly, but the benefits will be priceless. Increased power and explosion, along with the athleticism needed to perform this movement, will increase confidence in competition.

The final core lift is SQUATS. Full squats!!! Not sissy squats; quarter squats, leg extensions, or leg press. This is another exercise that has been associated with injury. Simply not true! Doing this exercise recklessly or without supervision HAS caused injury. Full squats are miserable, period! The amazing thing about squats is when you push them really hard for just 3 workouts, the strength gains are incredible.

How often have you heard an athlete say, "I don't do squats, they make you slow." Well, how does 6'1", 212 lbs., and a 4.5 forty sound! The next time he does a 580 lb. parallel squat, I'll tell him he's supposed to be slow. Not only can he outrun you, but he can dip his shoulder and run over you. Never let anyone tell you that you'll get slower by getting stronger. Never, never perform squats unsupervised. And never, never, never stop stretching or conditioning, because poor muscle elasticity and flexibility WILL slow you down.

If you can motivate yourself, get comfortable with the **UN**comfortable. The results will be tremendous. Over 18 years of experience has gone into this theory. Remember that more is not better - **BETTER IS BETTER!** Proper form, breathing, and control are the keys to success. **OVERTRAINING** is responsible for poor performance, muscle strains, tears, and peaks in weight training.

Sports Conditioning

AGILITY is "the ability to change direction without any loss of speed, strength, balance, or body control." Sports agility teaches an athlete the best method and techniques to move with the greatest speed and quickness, with the least amount of wasted movement and action. For example: In football - the great run, block, and tackle. In baseball - the big hit, catch, and steal. In basketball - getting open for the shot, the steal, the rebound. In volleyball - the great spike, the block, the save and so on.

The main ingredient is the display of the remarkable skills of agility. Implementing agility conditioning into your strength program will benefit you and your team and increase the potential for success. Although strength plays a major role in improving performance and preventing injury, speed and explosion are even more important. Every movement in organized athletics, whether it be the javelin throw, shot put, vertical jumping in basketball or volleyball, or instant bursts of speed in soccer and football. You must be EXPLOSIVE!

This type of training is the new wave of the future, and every competitive high school should include plyometrics in their sports conditioning programs. By tying together conditioning, agility and plyometrics, you'll make the complete package, and that's what college athletics is all about. These methods of training are the only way to increase strength in the fast twitch muscle fibers. Specialized exercises or devices are used to develop explosiveness, as a separate quality or in a special manner to duplicate the skill involved in your sport. Plyometric training is the key to developing maximum explosive power and speed of movement. Both which in turn are the key elements involved in sports.

Nutrition

"What you put into your body is what you get out of it." With that being said let's discuss 3 key nutritional points that will improve athleticism and also help you live a healthier lifestyle.

Hydration:

- Drink fluids throughout the day. Water should be your first choice when choosing a beverage.
- Drink things such as Gatorade only before, during and after an exercise session.
- Avoid calorie-ridden drinks such as soda, juices, etc.
- Caffeinated drinks lead to de-hydration.
- If you are thirsty you are already de-hydrated. During exercise or a sporting event you should sip a few ounces of water every 10-15 minutes.

Nutrients:

- Protein – Athletes can consume .75 – 1 gram of protein per pound of body weight. Example: An athlete weighing 200 pounds should consume 150-200 grams of protein daily.
- Fish, Chicken and lean beef are all healthy sources of protein.
- Other healthy sources of protein are tofu, beans, eggs, cottage cheese, yogurt and milk.
- Carbohydrates – This vital nutrient is the major supplier of fuel for the body.
- When choosing a carbohydrate it is important that the source contains at least 3 grams or more of fiber.
- Healthy sources of carbohydrates are found in fruits, vegetables, and grains.
- Fats – There are healthy types of fats that are critical to performance.
- Fish oil, flax seed oil, and nuts are all good sources of fats. Salad dressings, and butter are bad sources of fats.

Consistency:

- 5 of 6 meals in a day should be structured to reflect your nutritional goals.
- It is ok to overeat or indulge at times but just remember that you only get out of your body what you put into it.

Multi-Sport Participation

I'm going to make this easy for you! I just gave you $100 (or one scholarship) and I gave you an inventory list of car stereos (college recruits). Each one costs $100 and here are your options:

- am/fm receiver (one sport recruit)
- am/fm with CD player (two sport recruit)
- am/fm/xm, CD player w/iPod interface (three or four sport recruit)

I would take #3 and chances are the college coach is going to do the same. Do not limit yourself to one sport. College coaches want to see a well-rounded athlete. So, if you want to show them just how athletic you are, participate in as many sports as possible.

Camps & Clinics

Summer **CAMPS & CLINICS** are the best way to show college coaches what you have to offer. Make it a point to meet the coaching staff and get a first hand look at their program. While at a camp or clinic, there are virtually no restrictions on the type of contact you may have with the coaches and/or staff. This is the perfect opportunity to find out as much as you can and ask as many questions as possible. We always made it a point to find an athlete already on the team and ask them what they think of their program. Do this in private and away from the coach so the athlete is open and honest with you. You'll be surprised what you can find out from them. But keep in mind, you still may not accept any money or gifts of any kind whatsoever.

Mind of the Athlete®

By Jarrod Spencer, Psy.D. & Megan Cannon, Ph.D.

Clearer mind. Better performance. The clearer your mind is, the better you will perform. The idea seems logical; however, the mind is one of the commonly forgotten components in athletic training. Everyone can recall a moment where there were so many thoughts in your head that it felt next to impossible to accomplish anything. These moments are overwhelming, confusing, stressful, and not helpful when performing or competing. At Mind of the Athlete, our primary goal in working with athletes is helping them develop strategies to achieve a clearer mind, which leads to better performance athletically, academically, and interpersonally.

Mental health in our culture is a growing epidemic. According to the 2015 National College Health Assessment, 57.7% of college students reported experiencing overwhelming anxiety in the last year, which jumped 7% since 2013. Additionally, 35.3% of college students reported experiencing depression, which has increased 4% since 2013. When looking at athletes specifically, research suggests that 23.7% of college athletes report clinical levels of depression, with female athletes exhibiting nearly double the risk[1]. Consequently, we need to begin equipping student athletes with the skills to cope with the increasing stressors they face.

Dr. Brian Hainline, the Chief Medical Officer for the NCAA, stated that across the NCAA student athletes identified mental health as their primary concern[2].

1   Wolanin, A., Hong, E., Marks, D., Panchoo, K., & Gross, M. Prevalence of Clinically Elevated Symptoms in College Athletes and Differences by Gender and Sport. *British Journal of Sports Medicine,*
        2016, 50, 167-171.
2   Brown, G.T., Hainline, B., Kroshus, E., Wilfert, M. Mind, Body, and Sport: Understanding and Supporting Student-Athlete Mental Wellness. NCAA Publications, 2014.

At the NCAA annual meeting in January 2016 he said, "mental health is really, I think, going to be a game changer for the NCAA. My hope is that mental health is going to become as accessible to every student-athlete as an ankle sprain, and the NCAA is going to take a leadership role in telling the rest of the United States of America how to move away from the pathetic way it handles mental health. And it is pathetic." Guidelines were subsequently released as to how universities across the country can better manage mental health issues; however, similar guidelines do not exist at the high school level.

The culture of athletics has become increasingly more competitive. Athletes are pressured to specialize at younger ages, train more frequently, and compete year-round. Additionally, the landscape of securing a college scholarship has become increasingly more difficult. On top of the pressure, sports are emotional. Every athlete can identify moments in their career when they felt like they were on top of the world and others when they felt at the bottom.

To cope with the increasing pressure and emotions, the message typically sent within the world of athletics is "suck it up," or "push through it." Now to be fair, there are times athletes do need to do exactly that; however, if that is the only strategy we are teaching we are limiting their capability. Similarly to only doing one exercise during a workout, if we only have one option to managing emotions, we're limiting our full potential.

Sport psychology is the new edge in athletic training and competing. It is frequently said that sports are 90% mental; athletes are tapping into this now more than ever. Athletes and teams at collegiate, professional, and Olympic levels are utilizing it at an increasing rate.

With all this being said, has anyone ever taught you how the mind works? Picture an iceberg. A small portion, about 10% of the mass, exists above the surface of the water; the rest of the ice is hidden beneath. Your mind operates in a similar fashion. Your *conscious* mind, which represents the portion of the iceberg above water, includes those things you are consciously aware of at any given moment and this makes up about 10% of your mind. The other 90% below the water is your subconscious mind.

The waterline, which divides what we can see from what we cannot, represents your psychological defenses. A *psychological defense* is your mind's ability to block content in your subconscious mind from reaching the conscious mind. Its similar to a fence in your backyard, its purpose is to keep things out of your yard that you do not want coming in. Your psychological defenses allow you to better concentrate and focus at the present moment.

The subconscious mind is comprised of three layers. The bottom-most portion of the iceberg, buried deep beneath the water, is your *unconscious* mind. This area of the mind stores past experiences from the first few years of life. For instance, what did you do on your third birthday? This event occurred long ago and is not something you would likely recall. Sometimes intense emotional events and traumas, which can be too threatening to think about, can be pushed down and stored in this area. It's rare to remember events stored in the unconscious mind.

The middle layer of our subconscious is your *exconscious* mind. In this area, outdated or less useful memories are stored. For example, what did you do on your favorite birthday? It may take a few moments for your brain to recall these memories, but these events will be brought up into your conscious awareness and you can see them clearly. Athletes store many memories of athletic skill and development from practices and games here. Therefore, when memories in the exconscious can be accessed, it can help improve athletic performance.

The *preconscious* mind is the top layer of your subconscious that lies directly beneath the surface of the water and is the area most important to high performance. The preconscious mind stores memories that you can recall easily but are outside of your immediate awareness. Often times this area is filled with tasks, stressors, and experiences that you have coming up or have not yet dealt with. The preconscious mind does not have any sense of time. Therefore, you may have memories stored in this area that happened years ago, but to you it feels like it was yesterday.

As you go through your day, new information is continuously being processed through your conscious mind and it ends up in the preconscious mind. What happened at practice today? Who do you play this weekend? What homework do you have? Are you ready for the test this week? You and a friend got into an argument; what's going to happen? You're attracted to someone at school; do they like you back? Will your sore knee or ankle heal before the next game? Often times, you have more things in your preconscious mind than you realize.

Throughout the day when you have time to slow down, or maybe its during those moments when your head hits the pillow before you're asleep, you can become more aware of emotionally charged experiences in your preconscious mind. Can you think of a time where you were tossing and turning before falling asleep or having a difficult time concentrating in school due to unintentional thoughts coming into your mind? In these moments, things from your preconscious mind are coming up and entering your conscious awareness. This can be very distracting, tiring, and anxiety-provoking. When your preconscious mind becomes flooded with too many things, your psychological defenses begin to break down leaving you more vulnerable to things in our preconscious mind coming up and distracting you from your current awareness. Consequently, when your preconscious mind is clearer, your performance is better.

We must begin to equip athletes with strategies to help them strengthen their psychological defenses and clear out their preconscious mind. When this occurs, their mind is clearer and all of the positive qualities that make that athlete uniquely them from their personality to their ability to focus and perform has more room thrive.

At Mind of the Athlete, it is our mission to assist athletes in doing exactly this through our one-on-one coaching program, team consultation, speeches, and products. Our book, *Mind of the Athlete®: Clearer Mind, Better Performance*, is now available and is the practical first step for beginning mental training. Additionally, we have free online resources available through our website at www.mindoftheathlete.com, along with content posted to social media sites such as Twitter (@mindofathlete), Facebook (Mind of the Athlete) and Instagram (@mindoftheathlete). In fact, we have over 500 videos on our YouTube channel (youtube.com/mindoftheathlete), which cover a variety of sport psychology topics. Mental training is the next step in improving your performance: Are you ready to take it?

Jarrod Spencer, Psy.D.
drjarrod@mindoftheathlete.com
@Jarrod_Spencer

Megan Cannon, Ph.D.
Sports Psychologist
drmegan@mindoftheathlete.com
@DrMeganCannon
Mind of the Athlete®
3400 Bath Pike, Suite 302
Bethlehem, PA 18017
610.867.7770 (office)
www.mindoftheathlete.com
"Clearer Mind, Better Performance."

Scholarship Limits

Listed are the maximum number of athletic scholarships a university may award during each school year. Keep in mind that these numbers represent the total scholarships available per sport, for all classes, freshman through fifth year seniors. Remember, due to reduced budgets, colleges might not use the maximum limit that the NCAA established.

NCAA Scholarship Limits

Sport	Division I		Division II	
	Men's	Women's	Men's	Women's
Archery		5		9
Badminton		6		10
Baseball	11.7		9	
Basketball	13	15	10	10
Bowling		5		5
Equestrian		15		
Fencing	4.5	5	4.5	4.5
Field Hockey		12		6.3
Football	85*		36	
Golf	4.5	6	3.6	5.4
Gymnastics	6.3	12	5.4	6
Ice Hockey	18	18	13.5	18
Lacrosse	12.6	12	10.8	9.9
Rifle	3.6		3.6	
Rowing		20		20
Rugby		12		12
Skiing	6.3	7	6.3	6.3
Soccer	9.9	14	9	9.9
Softball		12		7.2
Squash		12		9
Swimming	9.9	14	8.1	8.1
Sync Swimming		5		5
Team Handball		10		12
Tennis	4.5	8	4.5	6
Track & XC	12.6	18	12.6	12.6
Volleyball	4.5	12	4.5	8
Water Polo	4.5	8	4.5	8
Wrestling	9.9		9	
* Division I-AA limit is 63				

42

NAIA & NJCAA Scholarship Limits

NAIA scholarships are similar to NCAA Division II, which are usually partial scholarships. NJCAA has guidelines as to how the scholarships may be awarded based on the Division of competition.

- Division I may grant the number of scholarships listed below.
- Division II may grant the number listed below, but are limited to tuition, fees and books.
- Division III may not offer athletic scholarships.

Sport	NAIA		NJCAA	
	Men's	Women's	Men's	Women's
Baseball	12		24	
Basketball	11 / 6	12 / 6	15	15
Cross Country	5	5	30	30
Football	24		85	
Golf	5	5	8	8
Ice Hockey			16	
Lacrosse			20	20
Soccer	12	12	18	18
Softball		10		24
Swimming	8	8	15	15
Tennis	5	5	9	9
Track	12	12	20	20
Volleyball	4.0	12		14
Water Polo	4.5	8	4.5	8
Wrestling	8		16	

NCAA Division I Recruiting Standards

Earlier in the "Evaluating Your Child's Talent" piece I mentioned my rule of thumb for determining which athletic level a child is most likely to achieve success. Remember this is just my barometer. College coaches have their own criteria when it comes to recruiting prospective student-athletes.

Not every athlete wants to compete at the Division I level. In fact, being a Division I athlete is a huge commitment. One must eat, sleep, and breathe one's sport, and a D-I athlete can plan on training throughout the year to stay in tip-top condition.

This section contains recruiting guidelines used by college coaches in each sport and includes the standards they use for recruiting athletes. But what if you never reach these standards? Should you give up on your dreams? Certainly not! If you are not a Division I athlete, consider Division II or III, or NAIA. Even within these divisions there are different levels of athletic programs / competition. I'm sure there is a level of athletics where you can compete. Use these guidelines as a way to measure your talent.

Baseball Recruiting Guidelines

The typical Division I baseball player is 'polished' and already has all the tools necessary to be successful as a freshman. As opposed to the Division II baseball player, the typical DI player needs far less development, if any. The position players possess at least 4 of the 5 measurable tools – hit for average, hit for power, arm strength, speed, and defensive abilities. The pitchers display a command of at least 3 pitches with high velocities. On average, they have the ability to throw many innings, and most often they are only used on the mound and rarely as position players.

Position	Division I	Division II	Division III
RH Pitchers	6'1", 180 lbs >1K Innings pitched ERA below 2.50 *Velocity - 88-90 MPH	6'0", 175 lbs 1K Innings pitched ERA below 3.00 *Velocity - 85 MPH	5'8", 155 lbs <1K Innings pitched ERA below 4.00 *Velocity - 81 MPH
LH Pitchers	6'1", 180 lbs >1K Innings pitched ERA below 2.50 *Velocity - 85-87 MPH	6'0", 175 lbs 1K Innings pitched ERA below 3.00 *Velocity - 85 MPH	5'8", 155 lbs <1K Innings pitched ERA below 4.00 *Velocity -79 MPH
Centerfielders	5'11", 170 lbs *60 Yd – 6.6 *Velocity - 86-87 MPH	5'10", 165 lbs *60 Yd – 6.8 or <	5'7", 140 lbs *60 Yd – 7.0 or <
Middle Infielders	5'11", 175 lbs *60 Yd – 6.9 *Velocity – 85+ MPH	5'9", 165 lbs *60 Yd – 6.9 or < *Velocity – 79+ MPH	5'7", 150 lbs *40 Yd – 4.9 or <
Catchers	5'10"+, 180 lbs *Pop Time <1.95	5'10", 180 lbs *Pop Time <2.0	5'8", 165 lbs *Pop Time <2.1
Corner Infielders	6'2", 200 lbs 8+ HR / 30+ RBI		

Preferred Grades
3.0+ GPA, 24+ ACT, 1000+ SAT (no scores needed for underclassmen)

Baseball by the Numbers

Division	Scholarships	Schools	Participants
NCAA Division I	11.7	299	10,195
NCAA Division II	9.0	274	8,603
NCAA Division III	0	389	11,588
NAIA	12	213	6,390
Others	0	42	
Junior College	24	394	11,820
Totals		1,555	
High School Statistics			
H. S. Athletes	478,029	H. S. Seniors	136,580

Key Baseball Websites

Baseball Coaches Association . . . . www.abca.org
NCAA Baseball . . . . www.ncaabaseball.com
HS Baseball Coaches . . . . www.baseballcoaches.org

Men's Basketball Recruiting Guidelines

Position	Division I	Division II	Division III
Center	Height 6'7" + / 10 PG Ability to run the floor (VG) Rebounding	Height 6'7" + / 10 PPG Ability to run the floor (VG) Rebounding	Height 6'5" + / 10 PPG Ability to run the floor (G) Rebounding skills
Power Forward	Height 6'7" + / 10 PPG Ability to run the floor (VG) Rebounding	Height 6'6" + / 10 PPG Ability to run the floor (VG) Rebounding	Height 6'4" + / 10 PPG Ability to run the floor (G) Rebounding skills
Small Forward	Height 6'4" + / 10 PPG Versatile scoring ability (G) Lateral quickness	Height 6'4" + / 10 PPG Versatile scoring ability (G) Lateral quickness	Height 6'2" + / 10 PPG Versatile scoring ability (G) Lateral quickness
Shooting Guard	Height 6'2" + / 10 PPG (E) Outside shot (VG) Lateral quickness (G) Ball handling skills (G) Passing skills	Height 6'1" + / 10 PPG (E) Outside shot (VG) Lateral quickness (G) Ball handling skills (G) Passing skills	Height 5'11" + / 10 PPG (E) Outside shot (G) Lateral quickness (G) Ball handling skills (G) Passing skills
Point Guard	Height 6'0" + / 10 PPG (E) Ball handling skills (E) Passing skills (E) Lateral quickness (E) Court awareness	Height 5'11" + / 10 PPG (VG) Ball handling (VG) Passing skills (VG) Lateral quickness (E) Court awareness	Height 5'8" + / 10 PPG (G) Ball handling skills (G) Passing skills (G) Lateral quickness (G) Court awareness
(E = Exceptional, VG = Very Good, G = Good)			

Preferred Grades

3.0+ GPA, 24+ ACT, 1000+ SAT (no scores needed for underclassmen)

Men's Basketball by the Numbers

Division	Scholarships	Schools	Participants
NCAA Division I	13.0	333	5,119
NCAA Division II	10.0	288	4,768
NCAA Division III	0	412	7,194
NAIA	12 / 6	265	3,975
Others	0	102	
Junior College	15	435	6,525
Totals		1,835	
High School Statistics			
H.S. Athletes	552,935	H. S. Seniors	157,981

Key Basketball Websites

NCAA Basketball . . . . www.ncaabasketball.net
Final Four . . . . www.finalfour.net
Hoops 4U www.hoops4U.com
AAU Basketball . . . . www.aauboysbasketball.org

Women's Basketball Recruiting Guidelines

Position	Division I	Division II	Division III
Center	Height 6'2" +/7 PPG Ability to run the floor (VG) Rebounding skills	Height 6'0" +/7 PPG Ability to run the floor (VG) Rebounding skills	Height 5'11" +/7 PPG Ability to run the floor (G) Rebounding skills
Power Forward	Height 6'0" +/7 PPG Ability to run the floor (VG) Rebounding skills	Height 5'11" +/7 PPG Ability to run the floor (VG) Rebounding skills	Height 5'9" +/7 PPG Ability to run the floor (G) Rebounding skills
Small Forward	Height 5'11" +/7 PPG Versatile scoring ability (G) Lateral quickness	Height 5'10" +/7 PPG Versatile scoring ability (G) Lateral quickness	Height 5'8" +/7 PPG Versatile scoring ability (G) Lateral quickness
Shooting Guard	Height 5'10" +/7 PPG (E) Outside shot (VG) Lateral quickness (G) Ball handling skills (G) Passing skills	Height 5'8" +/7 PPG (E) Outside shot (VG) Lateral quickness (G) Ball handling skills (G) Passing skills	Height 5'7" +/7 PPG (E)Outside shot (G) Lateral quickness (G) Ball handling skills (G) Passing skills
Point Guard	Height 5'8" +/7 PPG (E) Ball handling (E) Passing skills (E) Lateral quickness (E) Court awareness	Height 5'7" +/7 PPG (VG) Ball handling (VG) Passing skills (VG) Lateral quickness (E) Court awareness	Height 5'5" +/7 PPG (G) Ball handling skills (G) Passing skills (G) Lateral quickness (G) Court awareness
	(E = Exceptional, VG = Very Good, G = Good)		

Preferred Grades

3.0+ GPA, 24+ ACT, 1000+ SAT (no scores needed for underclassmen)

Women's Basketball by the Numbers

Division	Scholarships	Schools	Participants
NCAA Division I	15.0	331	4,765
NCAA Division II	10.0	289	4,291
NCAA Division III	0	436	6,251
NAIA	12 / 6	263	3,945
Others	0	85	
Junior College	15	390	5,850
Totals		1,794	
High School Statistics			
H. S. Athletes	449,540	H. S. Seniors	128,440

Key Basketball Websites

WB Coaches Association . . . . .www.wbca.org
Full Court Press. . . . . www.fullcourt.com
US Junior Nationals. . . . . .www.usjn.org
WB Magazine . . . . www.wbmagazine.com
AAU Basketball . . . . www.aaugirlsbasketball.org

Field Hockey Recruiting Guidelines

Division I	Division II	Division III
HS All-American Honors	HS All-State Honors	HS All-Region /
HS All-State Honors	HS All-Regional Honors	Conference Honors
Attends Major Tournaments	Attends Major Tournaments	HS Varsity Starter

Technical Skills Desired at all Levels	
Evaluation Skills	First step speed, Balance & agility. Ability to read plays, Strong Passing Ability, Field Vision
Developmental Skills	Passing, Hitting & Pushing, Trapping, Carrying the ball, Dribbling, Positioning in attack, Marking, Tackling, Covering, Leadership

Preferred Grades

3.0+ GPA, 24+ ACT, 1000+ SAT (no scores needed for underclassmen)

Field Hockey by the Numbers

Division	Scholarships	Schools	Participants
NCAA Division I	12.0	77	1,791
NCAA Division II	6.3	26	564
NCAA Division III	0	158	3,278
NAIA	0	0	
Others	0	0	
Junior College	0	0	
Totals		261	
High School Statistics			
H. S. Athletes	62,557	H. S. Seniors	17,873

Key Field Hockey Websites

US Field Hockey . . . . www.usfieldhockey.com
Planet Field Hockey. . . . . www.planetfieldhockey.com
Field Hockey Net . . . . www.fieldhockey.net
FH Coaches Association. . . . . www.eteamz.com/nfhca

Football Recruiting Guidelines

Pos.	Division I – A					Division I – AA & NJCAA				
	Ht.	Wt.	40	Bench	Squat	Ht.	Wt.	40	Bench	Squat
QB	6'2"	200	4.6	260	425	6'2"	190	4.7	250	385
RB	6'0"	210	4.5	315	415	5'11"	190	4.55	280	390
WR	6'2"	185	4.5	235	315	6'1"	185	4.6	225	295
TE	6'4"	240	4.7	300	440	6'4"	240	4.8	285	420
OL	6'4"	280	5.1	320	450	6'3"	275	5.2	305	425
DL	6'4"	250	4.8	315	450	6'3"	250	5.0	305	415
LB	6'1"	220	4.6	315	445	6'2"	220	4.7	300	435
DB	6'0"	185	4.5	260	385	6'0"	185	4.6	250	380
S	6'2"	200	4.6	270	405	6'2"	200	4.7	260	400

Pos.	Division II & NAIA					Division III				
	Ht.	Wt.	40	Bench	Squat	Ht.	Wt.	40	Bench	Squat
QB	6'2"	190	4.8	225	345	6'0"	175	4.8	205	315
RB	5'11"	190	4.6	270	375	5'10"	180	4.7	265	350
WR	6'1"	185	4.6	205	275	6'1"	180	4.7	200	265
TE	6'3"	220	4.85	275	415	6'2"	215	4.9	270	405
OL	6'3"	290	5.4	300	410	6'2"	275	5.5	295	405
DL	6'2"	260	5.1	305	405	6'1"	250	5.2	295	395
LB	6'0"	210	4.7	295	405	5'11"	195	4.75	275	395
DB	5'11"	185	4.65	250	380	5'10"	180	4.7	240	295

Preferred Grades

3.0+ GPA, 24+ ACT, 1000+ SAT (no scores needed for underclassmen)

Football by the Numbers

Division	Scholarships	Schools	Participants
NCAA Division IA	85	120	13,758
NCAA Division IAA	63	119	11,900
NCAA Division II	38	154	15,764
NCAA Division III	0	239	22,813
NAIA	24	92	9,200
Others	0	4	
Junior College	85	71	7,100
Totals		799	
High School Statistics			
H. S. Athletes	1,108,286	H. S. Seniors	316,653

Key Football Websites

NCAA Football. . . . . .www.ncaafootball.net
College Football News. . . . . www.collegefootballnew.com
American Football Coaches . . . . www.afca.com
College Football. . . . . www.collegefootball.com

Golf Recruiting Guidelines

	Men's	Women's
Division I	Handicap: Scratch or better 18 Hole Average – 73 or less Top Finishes in Nat'l Tournaments Competes in Local Tournaments	Handicap: Equal to or <5 18 Hole Average – 78 or less Top Finishes in Nat'l Tourneys Competes in Local Tournaments
Division II and Women's NAIA	Handicap: Equal to or <1 18 Hole Average: 74 or less Competes in Nat'l Tournaments Competes in Local Tournaments	Handicap: Equal to or <10 18 Hole Average – 85 or less Top Finishes in Nat'l Tournaments Competes in Local Tournaments
Division III and Men's NAIA	Handicap: Equal to or <3 18 Hole Average – 75 or less Preferred Tournaments Competes in Local Tournaments	Handicap: Equal to or <15 18 Hole Average – 95 or less Top Finishes in Nat'l Tournaments Competes in Local Tournaments

Preferred Grades

3.0+ GPA, 24+ ACT, 1000+ SAT (no scores needed for underclassmen)

Golf by the Numbers

Division	Scholarships		Schools		Participants	
	Men	Women	Men	Women	Men	Women
NCAA Division I	4.5	6.0	291	243	2,960	2,047
NCAA Division II	3.6	5.4	210	134	2,280	973
NCAA Division III	0	0	284	164	1,267	1,076
NAIA	5.0	5.0	181	139	1,482	973
Others	0	0	25	6		
Junior Colleges	8.0	8.0	215	88		
Totals			1,206	772		

High School Statistics		
	Men	Women
High School Athletes	159,958	69,243
High School Seniors	45,702	19,784

Key Golf Websites

College Golf Foundation . . . . www.cgfgolf.org
Golf Coaches Association . . . . .www.collegiategolf.com
College Golf. . . . . www.golfstat.com
USGA. . . . . www.usga.org

Gymnastics Recruiting Guidelines

D-I & D-II Recruiting Athletic Guidelines

Participation Level	
Level 10 – Division I	Level 9 – Low Division I, Division II and Division III
Developmental Skills	
Vault	Uneven Bars
Balance Beam	Floor
Mounts	Landings

Events for coaches to make evaluations

USA Gymnastics	Federation of International Gymnastics
Local Qualifiers	US Association of Independent Gymnastic Clubs
State Championships	Regional Qualifiers / Championships
AAU / Junior Olympics	National Championships

Preferred Grades

3.0+ GPA, 24+ ACT, 1000+ SAT (no scores needed for underclassmen)

Gymnastics the Numbers

Division	Scholarships		Schools		Participants	
	Men	Women	Men	Women	Men	Women
NCAA Division I	6.3	17.8	15	61	304	1,085
NCAA Division II	5.4	19	0	6	0	114
NCAA Division III	0	18.2	1	15	21	1,492
NAIA	0	0	0	0	0	0
Others	0	0	0	0	0	0
Junior Colleges	0	0	0	0	0	0
Totals	11.7	55	16	82	325	2,691

High School Statistics		
	Men	Women
High School Athletes	122	1,550

Key Gymnastics Websites

USA Gymnastics . . . . www.usa-gymnastics.org
College Gymnastics . . . . www.toroester.com/gym
Federation of International Gymnastics . . . . . www.gif-gymnastics.com
USAIGC . . . . .www.usaigc.com

Ice Hockey Recruiting Guidelines

Qualifications	
Men's	**Women's**
Prep Schools USHL NAHL EJHL CJAHL USA Hockey Development Camps	Prep Schools Junior Women's Hockey League USA Hockey Development Camps

Preferred Grades

3.0+ GPA, 24+ ACT, 1000+ SAT (no scores needed for underclassmen)

Ice Hockey by the Numbers

Division	Scholarships		Schools		Participants	
	Men	Women	Men	Women	Men	Women
NCAA Division I	18.0	18.0	58	35	1,632	837
NCAA Division II	13.5	18.0	7	2	218	52
NCAA Division III	0	0	73	46	2,156	1,007
ACHA	0	0	336	41		
Junior Colleges	16.0	0	11	0		
Totals			485	124		

High School Statistics		
	Men	Women
H.S. Athletes	36,667	8,621
H..S. Seniors	10,476	2,463

Key Ice Hockey Websites

College Hockey . . . . www.collegehockey.org
USA Hockey . . . . www.usahockey.com
NCAA Ice Hockey . . . . www.ncaaicehockey.com

Lacrosse Recruiting Guidelines

Division I	Division II	Division III
All-American Honors HS All-State Honors US Lacrosse Reg'l Team Attends Major Tourneys	High School All-Region / Conference Honors Attends Major Tourneys HS Varsity Starter	High School All-Region / Conference Honors HS Varsity Starter

Technical Skills by Position			
Attackers	Midfielders	Defensemen	Goalie
Men's Ht.: 5'7" +	Men's Ht.: 5'10" +	Men's Ht.: 5'10" +	Men's Ht.: 5'9"+
Strong Scoring	Strong Passing	Take-away Checking	Reaction Time
Field Vision	Scoring	Stick Skills	Body Positioning
Passing	Size	Strength	Clearing Ability
Size / Speed	Speed	Size	Arc and Angle
Quickness	Quickness	Speed	Stick Handling

Preferred Grades

3.0+ GPA, 24+ ACT, 1000+ SAT (no scores needed for underclassmen)

Lacrosse by the Numbers

Division	Scholarship		Schools		Participants	
	Men	Women	Men	Women	Men	Women
NCAA Division I	12.6	12.0	57	85	2,507	2,317
NCAA Division II	10.8	9.9	35	48	1,258	919
NCAA Division III	0	0	151	180	5,135	3,594
Others	0	0	2	1		
Junior Colleges	20	20	27	18	540	360
Totals			272	332		
High School Statistics						
	Men			Women		
H. S. Athletes	82,860			61,086		
H. S. Seniors	23,674			17,453		

Key Lacrosse Websites

360 Lacrosse............................ www.360lacrosse.com
US Lacrosse .... www.lacrosse.org
Women's Lacrosse Coaches Association.............. www.iwlca.org
Inside Lacrosse .... www.insidelacrosse.com

Rowing / Crew Recruiting Guidelines

2000 M Ergometer	Heavyweight High Level	Heavyweight Low Level	Lightweight High Level	Lightweight Low Level
Men's	6:20 to 7:00	7:00 to 10:00	7:00 to 7:30	7:30 to 12:00
Women's	7:20 to 8:00	8:00 to 11:30	8:00 to 8:30	8:30 to 15:00

Preferred Grades

3.0+ GPA, 24+ ACT, 1000+ SAT (no scores needed for underclassmen)

Rowing by the Numbers

Division	Scholarship		Schools		Participants	
	Men	Women	Men	Women	Men	Women
NCAA Division I	0	20.0	28	86	1,430	5,441
NCAA Division I Club	0	0	62	25		
NCAA Division II	0	20.0	4	15	96	416
NCAA Division II Club	0	0	9	5		
NCAA Division III	0	0	31	43	906	1,353
NCAA Division III Club	0	0	21	22		
Totals			155	196		
High School Statistics						
H. S. Women Athletes	2,685		H. S. Women Seniors		767	

* Notes: Schools listed under Club represent schools that have only club rowing. Schools that have Varsity and club rowing are not included.

Key Rowing Websites

USA Rowing .... www.usrowing.org
Rowing Links .... www.rowinglinks.com
Crew Coaches Association .... www.collegerowcoach.org

Soccer Recruiting Guidelines

Most Division I soccer players have club experience and play for a high level premier/ elite club team that attends out of state tournaments. The majority, but NOT ALL Division I players have ODP experience at the state level or higher. High level club tournament play and ODP soccer come closest to mirroring the college game, and this is where most collegiate scouting takes place. Nearly 100% of all Division I soccer players who played for their high school teams have earned at least All-Conference recognition. Most have also received All-District, All-State and All-Region honors.

Division I	Division II	Division III / NAIA
National / Regional / State ODP Team ESP Camp Club Experience High School All-American Honors	ODP Experience - Tryouts Club Experience Varsity Starter	Club Experience Varsity Starter

Events for Coaches to Make Evaluations

Disney Showcase	Score at the Shore
Surf Cup	Jefferson Cup
Blue Chip Tournament	Crossroads Showcase
Celtic Cup	Mustang Invitational
YMS Columbus Day	WAGS Cup

Preferred Grades

3.0+ GPA, 24+ ACT, 1000+ SAT (no scores needed for underclassmen)

Soccer by the Numbers

Division	Scholarships		Schools		Participants	
	Men	Women	Men	Women	Men	Women
NCAA Division I	9.9	14.0	198	310	5,556	7,995
NCAA Division II	9.0	9.9	179	225	4,801	5,344
NCAA Division III	0	0	401	424	10,674	9,383
NAIA	12.0	12.0	218	222	5,104	5,106
Others	0	0	71	44		
Junior Colleges	18.0	18.0	216	180	4,968	4,140
Totals			1,283	1,405		
High School Statistics						
	Men			Women		
H. S. Athletes	383,561			348,545		
H. S. Seniors	109,589			99,584		

Key Soccer Websites

NSCAA . . . . www.nscaa.com
US Soccer . . . . www.socceramerica.com
College Soccer . . . . www.collegesoccernews.com

Softball Recruiting Guidelines

Position	Division I	Division II	Division III
RH Pitchers	5'9" ERA 1.00 or < *Speed. - 60-63 MPH	5'7" ERA 1.50 < *Speed – 58+ MPH	5'6" ERA 2.00 < *Speed – 55+ MPH
Centerfielders	5'7", 135 lbs Home to 1st – 2.8 Batting Avg. – .400+	5'5", 130 lbs Home to 1st – 2.9 Batting Avg. – .360+	5'4", 130 lbs Home to 1st – 3.1 Batting Avg. – .330+
Middle Infielders	5'6", 135 lbs Home to 1st – 2.8 Stolen Bases – 10+	5'5", 135 lbs Home to 1st – 2.9 Stolen Bases – 10+	5'4", 125 lbs Home to 1st – 3.1 Stolen Bases – 8+
Catchers	5'8", 160 lbs *Pop Time <1.8 Home to 1st -<3.0	5'4", 150 lbs *Pop Time <1.9 Home to 1st -<3.1	5'4", 140 lbs *Pop Time <2.0 Home to 1st -<3.2
Corner Infielders	5'7", 145 lbs Home to 1st – 2.9 RBIs – 20+ Home Runs – 2+	5'6", 145 lbs Home to 1st – 3.0 RBIs – 15+ Home Runs – 1+	5'5", 135 lbs Home to 1st – 3.1 RBIs – 15+ Home Runs – 1+

Preferred Grades

3.0+ GPA, 24+ ACT, 1000+ SAT (no scores needed for underclassmen)

Softball by the Numbers

Division	Scholarships	Schools	Participants
NCAA Division I	12.0	276	5,285
NCAA Division II	7.2	268	4,905
NCAA Division III	0	408	6,954
NAIA	10.0	210	4,200
Others	0	32	
Junior College	24.0	358	7,160
Totals		1,552	
High School Statistics			
H. S. Athletes	371,293	H. S. Seniors	106,084

Key Softball Websites

ASA Softball . . . . www.softball.org
NSA Softball . . . . www.playnsa.com
USA Softball . . . . .www.usasoftball.com
Softball Net . . . . www.softball.net
The Softball Site . . . . www.thesoftballsite.com

Swimming Recruiting Guidelines

Men's Guidelines					
Event	High D-I	Low D-I	High D-II	Low D-II	D-III
50 Freestyle	<21.4	<22.0	<22.0	<23.5	<24.0
500 Freestyle	<4:35	<4:45	<4:50	<5:00	<5:05
100 Backstroke	<52.0	<55.0	<55.0	<57.0	<59.0
100 Breaststroke	<57.0	<1:01.0	<1:01.0	<1:04.0	<1:06.0
100 Fly	<51.0	<54.0	<56.0	<57.0	<59.0
200 IM	<1:55.0	<2:01.0	<2:02.0	<2:05.0	<2:08.0
Women's Guidelines					
Event	High D-I	Low D-I	High D-II	Low D-II	D-III
50 Freestyle	<24.0	<25.0	<25.5	<26.5	<28.0
500 Freestyle	<5:00.0	<5:06.0	<5:10.0	<5:18.0	<5:32.0
100 Backstroke	<57.0	<1:00.0	<1:00.5	<1:02.0	<1:06.0
100 Breaststroke	<1:08.0	<1:12.0	<1:13.0	<1:15.0	<1:17.0
100 Fly	<55.0	<59.0	<1:00.0	<1:02.0	<1:07.0
200 IM	<2:02.0	<2:10.0	<2:11.0	<2:16.0	<2:24.0

Preferred Grades

3.0+ GPA, 24+ ACT, 1000+ SAT (no scores needed for underclassmen)

Swimming by the Numbers

Division	Scholarships		Schools		Participants	
	Men	Women	Men	Women	Men	Women
NCAA Division I	9.9	14.0	139	193	3,670	5,155
NCAA Division II	8.1	8.1	56	72	1,080	1,392
NCAA Division III	0	0	197	242	3,632	4,691
NAIA	8.0	8.0	21	28	420	560
Others	0	0	2	3		
Junior Colleges	15.0	15.0	17	18	340	360
Totals			486	502		
High School Statistics						
	Men			Women		
H. S. Athletes	111,896			147,197		
H. S. Seniors	31,970			42,056		

Key Swimming Websites

USA Swimming . . . . www.usa-swimming.org
ASCA Online . . . . www.swimmingcoach.org
Swim News . . . . www.swimnews.com
CSCAA . . . . www.cscaa.org

Tennis Recruiting Guidelines

	Division I	Division II	Division III
Men's	Height – Average 6'1" 4 Years Varsity State Champion National Top 100 Sectional Top 20 Ext Personal Training	Height – Average 5'11" 3 Years Varsity State Qualifier National Top 600 Sectional Top 40 Yrs Personal Training	Height – Average 5'11" 3 Years Varsity State Qualifier National Top 600 Sectional Top 250 Yrs Personal Training
Women's	Height – Average 5'6" 4 Years Varsity State Champion National Top 100 Sectional Top 30 Competes on National Level Ext Personal Training	Height – Average 5'5" 3 Years Varsity State Qualifier National Top 500 District Top 50 Sect. Rank – Desired Yrs Personal Training	Height – Average 5'5" 2+ Years Varsity Team Captain District Top 50 Sect. Rank – Prefrd Yrs Personal Training

Preferred Grades

3.0+ GPA, 24+ ACT, 1000+ SAT (no scores needed for underclassmen)

Tennis by the Numbers

Division	Scholarship		Schools		Participants	
	Men	Women	Men	Women	Men	Women
NCAA Division I	4.5	8.0	258	311	2,680	2,891
NCAA Division II	4.5	6.0	168	220	1,619	2,004
NCAA Division III	0	0	325	371	3,551	3,826
NAIA	5.0	5.0	107	123	1,070	1,230
Others	0	0	10	15		
Junior Colleges	9.0	9.0	80	92	938	1,117
Totals			948	1,132		

High School Statistics		
	Men	Women
H. S. Athletes	156,285	172,455
H. S. Seniors	44,652	49,272

Key Tennis Websites

USTA . . . . www.usta.org
College Tennis . . . . www.collegetennisonline.com
Jr. Tennis . . . . www.collegeandjuniortennis.com

Track and Field Recruiting Guidelines

Event	Division I		Division II		Division III / NAIA	
	M	W	M	W	M	W
55M	6.4	7.11	6.6	7.5	6.8	7.8
60M	6.8	7.65	6.95	7.95	7.3	8.2
55MH	7.4		7.65		8.0	
60MH	7.8	8.6	8.07	9.2	8.3	9.5
110M High Hurdles	13.95	14.5	14.9	15.2	15.5	15.5
300M Hurdles	37.0	43.1	40.0	46.5	42.0	48.5
400M Hurdles	51.0	60.0	54.5	63.0	56.00	1:07
100M	10.5	11.9	10.0	12.5	11.0	12.5
200M	21.25	24	22.00	26.2	22.15	25.8
400M	47.5	54.5	49.0	59.0	49.5	59.5
800M	1:52	2:10	1:57	2:20	1:57	2:20
1500M	3:55	4:40	4:00	4:50	4:05	4:40
1600M	4:15	5:00	4:30	5:15	4:30	5:30
3000M Steeple	9:34	10:45	9:45	11:00	9:45	11:40
3200M	9:10	11:00	9:30	11:30	9:45	11:50
High Jump	7'0"	5'10"	6'4"	5'4"	6'1"	5'1"
Pole Vault	16'6"	12'6"	15'6"	10'6"	15'0"	10'6"
Long Jump	24'6"	19'6"	22'6"	17'0"	21'9"	18'0"
Triple Jump	51'0"	40'0"	45'0"	35'0"	44'6"	36'0"
Shot Put	60'10"	45'0"	50'0"	38'0"	50'0"	40'0"
Discus	185'0"	149'0"	150'0"	120'0"	150'0"	120'0"
Javelin	210'0"	140'0"	170'0"	120'0"	160'0"	110'0"
Hammer	210'0"	170'0"	170'0"	140'0"	160'0"	136'0"
Decathlon	7000		6000		5800	
Heptathlon		5000		4500		3600

Preferred Grades

3.0+ GPA, 24+ ACT, 1000+ SAT (no scores needed for underclassmen)

Track by the Numbers

Division	Scholarship		Schools		Participants	
	Men	Women	Men	Women	Men	Women
NCAA Division I	12.6	18.0	269	307	10,266	11,230
NCAA Division II	12.6	12.6	162	174	5,052	4,451
NCAA Division III	0	0	267	274	8,161	6,682
NAIA	12.0	12.0	133	135	2,340	2,460
Others	0	0	2	3		
Junior Colleges	20.0	20.0	78	82		
Totals			911	975		
High School Statistics						
	Men			Women		
H. S. Athletes	548,821			447,520		
H. S. Seniors	156,806			127,862		

Cross Country Recruiting Guidelines

Men's Guidelines						
Event	Division I		Division II		Division III / NAIA	
	Tier 1	Tier 2	Tier 1	Tier 2	Tier 1	Tier 2
5,000M (5K)	15.00	15:50	16:20	17:15	17:00	18:00
10,000M	31.00	35:00	34:00	36:00	35:00	40:00
Women's Guidelines						
Event	Division I		Division II		Division III	
	Tier 1	Tier 2	Tier 1	Tier 2	Tier 1	Tier 2
5,000M (5K)	18:30	18:50	18:55	21:00	21:00	23:00
10,000M	35:00	36:00	36:00	40:00	42:30	46:00

Preferred Grades

3.0+ GPA, 24+ ACT, 1000+ SAT (no scores needed for underclassmen)

Swimming by the Numbers

Division	Scholarship		Schools		Participants	
	Men	Women	Men	Women	Men	Women
NCAA Division I	12.6	18.0	296	321	4,390	5,203
NCAA Division II	12.6	12.6	245	275	2,851	3,111
NCAA Division III	0	0	357	371	4,961	4,989
NAIA	5.0	5.0	177	185		
Others	0	0	20	21		
Junior Colleges	30.0	30.0	185	184		
Totals			1,261	1,348		

High School Statistics		
	Men	Women
H. S. Athletes	216,085	183,376
H. S. Seniors	61,739	52,393

Key Track & Cross Country Websites

HS Runner . . . . www.highschoolrunner.com
USA Track & Field . . . . www.usatf.org
Runner's World . . . . www.runnerwsworld.com
Running USA . . . . www.runningusa.org

Volleyball Recruiting Guidelines

Men's	Division I	Division II	Division III
	2 – 4x Varsity Starter Nat'l / Elite Club Exp.	2x Varsity Starter Nat'l / Elite Club Exp.	Varsity Starter Club Exp.
Libero	Ht. 6'0" (5'8" – 6'2") Vertical – 24"+	Ht. 6'0" (5'8" – 6'2") Vertical – 24"+	Ht. 5'10" (5'8" – 6'2") Vertical – 24"+
MH	Ht. 6'7" (6'5" – 7'0") Appr Touch – 11'6"	Ht. 6'7" (6'5" – 7'0") Appr Touch – 11'0"	Ht. 6'5" (6'3" – 6'7") Appr Touch – 11'6"
OH / RS	Ht. 6'6" (6'4" – 6'10") Appr Touch – 11'0"	Ht. 6'4" (6'3" – 6'6") Appr Touch – 10'10"	Ht. 6'2" (6'0" – 6'4") Appr Touch – 11'0"
Setter	Ht. 6'3" (6'1" – 6'5") Appr Touch – 10'8"	Ht. 6'3" (6'1" – 6'5") Appr Touch – 10'6"	Ht. 6'1" (6'0" – 6'5") Appr Touch – 10'6"
Women's	**Division I**	**Division II**	**Division III**
	3+ Yrs. Varsity 5+ Yrs. Club Exp. Nat'l Tourn. Plcemnt	2+Yrs. Varsity 3+ Yrs. Club Exp. Nat'l Tourn. Exp.	1-2 Years Varsity 2+ Years Club Exp. Attend Nat'l Tourn.
Libero	Ht. 5'5" – 6'0", 125 lbs Vertical – 28"+	Ht. 5'2" – 5'8" Vertical – 22"+	Ht. 5'0" – 5'8" Vertical – 20"+
MH	Ht. 6'0" – 6'4", 155lbs Appr Touch – 10'0"	Ht. 5'10" – 6'2" Appr Touch – 9'8"+	Ht. 5'9" – 6'1" Appr Touch – 9'6"
OH / RS	Ht. 5'11" – 6'2", 140lbs Appr Touch – 9'10"	Ht. 5'8" – 5'11" Appr Touch – 9'6"+	Ht. 5'9" – 5'10" Appr Touch – 9'4"
Setter	Ht. 5'8" – 6'1", 130 lbs Appr Touch – 9'5"	Ht. 5'7" – 5'10" Appr Touch – 9'2"+	Ht. 5'4" – 5'10" Appr Touch – 9'0"+

Preferred Grades

3.0+ GPA, 24+ ACT, 1000+ SAT (no scores needed for underclassmen)

Volleyball by the Numbers

Division	Scholarship		Schools		Participants	
	Men	Women	Men	Women	Men	Women
NCAA Division I	4.5	12.0	22	317	456	4,650
NCAA Division II	4.5	8.0	13	276	238	4,020
NCAA Division III	0	0	47	423	604	6,045
NAIA	4.0	8.0	17	251	255	3,312
Others	0	0		86		
Junior Colleges	0	14.0		297		
Totals			99	1,651		
High School Statistics						
	Men			**Women**		
H. S. Athletes	46,780			397,968		
H. S. Seniors	13,366			113,705		

Key Volleyball Websites

USA Volleyball . . . . www.usavolleyball.org

Wrestling Recruiting Guidelines

Division I	Division II	Division III / NAIA
State Champ or Multiple Placer	State Placer	District Placer
Junior Nat'l Champ or Placer	District or Regional Champ	2X Varsity Starter
Won or Place @ Tourney of Champions	3X Varsity Starter	Win or Place in HS Tournaments
4X Varsity Starter	Winner of HS Tourn.	
Placed in Top Tourn.	Experience in Greco & FS	

Events for Coaches to Make Evaluations

Delaware Beast of the East

Five-Counties Invitational (CA)

Easton – Phillipsburg Wrestling Duals

Iron Man Invitational (OH)

Minnesota Christmas Tournament

Reno Tournament of Champions

Powerade Christmas Tournament

Manheim Tournament

Clovis Buchanan Invitational (CA)

Virginia Duals

Preferred Grades

3.0+ GPA, 24+ ACT, 1000+ SAT (no scores needed for underclassmen)

Wrestling by the Numbers

Division	Scholarship	Schools	Participants
NCAA Division I	9.9	86	2,648
NCAA Division II	9.0	45	1,318
NCAA Division III	0	92	2,334
NAIA	6.0	35	910
Others	0	3	
Junior College	16.0	44	
Totals		305	
High School Statistics			
H. S. Athletes			259,688
H. S. Seniors			74,197

Key Wrestling Websites

National High School Coaches . . . . www.nhsca.com/wrestling
Intermat . . . . www.intermatwrestling.com
World of Wrestling . . . . www.worldofwrestling-roller.com
Wrestling USA . . . . www.wrestlingusa.com
The Wrestling Mall. . . . . www.thewrestlingmall.com

Goal Setting

As an athlete, it is impossible to become the best or achieve anything without having focus **and direction**. The way you stay focused is by setting **GOALS**. First, you must determine what you want to accomplish, then, what effort it will take on your part to achieve it. The following is an example of how goals are formed.

If you took five different high school female athletes and asked them what they each wanted out of their athletic careers, you might get answers like these.

Girl #1 – I love playing soccer and I don't want my career to end when I graduate from high school. I realize that I can never be a scholarship athlete in college, but I just want to compete in college at some level.

Girl #2 – Last year I placed 5th in swimming at the district meet. I would like to make it to states before I graduate.

Girl #3 – I'm a sophomore and I've been playing basketball for five years. When I was in junior high school, I was able to compete with girls my own age, but now, I don't match up well physically with juniors and seniors. I need to get stronger so I can hold my own under the basket.

Girl #4 – When my sister was in high school, she was All-Conference in track. She even placed 4th in the state her senior year. She was recruited by a lot of big schools, but when the time came for scholarship offers, no one came knocking. At the time, I didn't understand why but later I found out her grades weren't very good. She only carried a 2.3 GPA and had sub-par SAT scores. She thought she could rely on her athletic ability to get her into college, so she was lazy in the classroom. I don't want that to happen to me. I want to have a 3.0 GPA or higher and score at least an 1100 on the SAT's.

Girl #5 – Ever since I was a little girl, all I ever thought about was playing softball at UCLA. I've worked hard in the classroom as well as on the field to give myself the best opportunity to make it. My parents didn't go to college so they don't know much about the recruiting process. I don't want to make any mistakes along the way or leave any stones unturned. I need to find someone that can help me plan my road to success

Some might call these dreams, others goals. Truth is, there's a difference between dreams and goals. Dreams are things we wish for and hope will happen, while goals are things we want to accomplish that are either within our grasp or at least very possible. There are two types of goals: **short term and long term**. Every athlete that wants to be successful must have both.

Start by creating a list of **SHORT-TERM GOALS,** things you want to improve over a period of days, weeks or even a few months. Then, make a very detailed and precise **SUB-LIST,** or plan of action next to each goal. This sub-list will act as a blueprint to accomplish each goal.

Next, create a list of **LONG-TERM GOALS.** Things you want to improve over a longer period of time such as several months or even a year or longer. Then, make a sub-list next to each of these. Again, you are creating a blueprint for SUCCESS! Below, I've given you an example of what your list of goals and sub-lists should look like.

Short-Term Goals

I want to get stronger so I can be more effective under the basket.

- Do 50 sit-ups and push-ups every morning. Increase the reps by 10 each week.
- Run fifteen - 20 yard sprints every other day for short-burst energy.
- Ask our strength coach to create a weightlifting/conditioning program for me.
- I want to carry a 3.0 GPA and score a minimum 1100 on the SAT's.
- Find a student/tutor to help me with math (my weakest subject).
- Ask my teachers if I can do extra credit work to increase my GPA.
- Purchase a "practice software program" to help build my SAT test skills.

Long-Term Goals

I want to qualify for the state meet (swimming) before I graduate in 2 years.

- Build up stamina for my longer events.
- Increase training by 30 minutes a day, and 2 hours more on the weekends.
- Expose myself to tougher competition by entering several National Open meets.
- I want to play softball at UCLA
- Be prepared mentally and physically by the time I'm a junior.
- Ask my high school coach to market and promote me to the colleges.
- Work hard in the classroom to separate myself academically from other prospects.

My son, Coy, used to write his goals on paper then tape them to the ceiling above his bed. Every night before he went to sleep, and every morning when he woke up, the first and last thing he saw each day was his GOALS! It's important to see these goals everyday so you don't lose focus or become distracted. Distractions can come in the form of an injury, a problem in school, a death in the family, or just a bad decision on your part. Yes, that will happen many times along the way. Just make sure you learn from each one. Now that you have your blueprint for success, what are you waiting for?

Tips for Goal Setting

- Set specific, objective goals. By objective, we mean that the goal must be stated in measurable quantitative terms. For example, a tennis player might set a goal of hitting 70% good first serves. You must avoid subjective goals that are based on the opinion of an evaluator, such as most valuable player. If you want to be named the MVP at the end of the season, that's fine, just don't use it as a goal.
- Use a combination of long-term and short-term goals. Short-term goals provide stepping stones toward achieving the long-term goal. Both are necessary.

- Evaluate your progress frequently. You want to know how you are progressing towards achieving the goals you have set. Relatively frequent evaluation will help keep you motivated once you see progress or it may encourage you to work harder if you are behind schedule.

- Set reachable and challenging goals. This applies to every goal set. You must find the middle ground between hard, unachievable goals and easy, non-motivating goals. This is a good place for a coach or parent to help you in setting goals. When you are involved in setting your goals you feel responsible for the goals and will be motivated to achieve them. If your coach or parent sets the goals for you, you may not feel any sense of ownership and not be as concerned whether or not you achieve those goals. Parents, remember you cannot relive your life though your child; it is their goal not yours.

"Food for Thought"

"The most important thing about goals is having them."

Geoffrey Albert

"If you aim at nothing, you'll hit it every time."

Unknown

"Goals that are not written down are just wishes."

Unknown

"Write it down, Written goals have a way of transforming wishes into wants; can'ts into cans; dreams into plans; and plans into reality. Don't just think it -- Ink it!"

Unknown

"There's only one thing in this world that can keep you from achieving your goals, that would be -- YOU."

Unknown

MARKETING

It sounds like we're going to talk about selling books, or furniture, or a new cleaning product. Actually, the product we're talking about marketing is **YOU**, the high school student-athlete.

First, ask your high school coach what level of college athletics you are most suited for, NCAA Division I, II or III, NAIA or Junior College. It's important to be honest and realistic about your talent and abilities. For instance, would you rather sit the bench for four years at an NCAA Division I school or play three years at a Division II school?

Next, you have to understand the odds you're up against. Each year Stanford University Football sends out approximately 3000 letters to prospective juniors in high school all across the country. But they may only have about 19 scholarships to give out that year. These figures are typical although some sports have a lot fewer scholarships to offer than others. But don't be discouraged, we're going to show you how to increase your odds of getting one of those hard-to-get college athletic scholarships. When it comes to marketing your student-athlete, you really have three options.

The Three Options of Marketing

Option #1 - Cross your fingers, kneel by your bed, and pray that some college or university will find your son or daughter.

If you believe your son or daughter is good enough that colleges will be knocking down your doors when recruiting time comes, then this may be your choice. But I would like to make one point first.

When my son was in high school, he was a top high school prospect in both football and wrestling and became very highly recruited. I decided to market him anyway. My thoughts were this. If I don't do anything and he receives two offers his senior year that would be GREAT! But what if I did some things to get his name, face, and talent in front of the college coaches and showed them what he brought to the table. In doing that, perhaps I could increase his options and scholarship offers. Instead of getting those two offers his senior year, what if he received six offers by April 1st of his junior year? That is exactly what happened. By marketing him to college coaches, I made it easier for them to evaluate his talent. This led to early offers and accelerated the recruiting process for my son. So give serious thought before using option #1.

Option #2 - Do it yourself using our "Four-Step Marketing Plan".

This is the option I chose for my son. Now again let me preface this by saying I had a VERY GOOD PRODUCT TO MARKET!

- All-American in football (started both ways as a freshman)
- Co-captained Pennsylvania's BIG 33 All-star team.
- 2 - time State runner-up in wrestling (career record 120-11)
- Earned 12 varsity letters in four years
- Scored close to 1200 on the SAT's
- 3.6 GPA
- Ranked in the top 1/5th of a very high academic high school class

Are you getting the picture? I want to be sure you understand what I had to work with and why I chose this route.

I started by creating an "Athletic Recruiting Profile" and sent one to each college coach that sent him a recruiting letter. He received letters from over 50 Division I colleges. I also sent packets to schools he was interested in but were not sending letters yet. In all, I probably sent out a total of 70 packets during his first 3 years in high school. That's right! I started during his freshman year and continued through his junior year. Each packet cost me an average of $20 including postage. That did not, however, account for all the time and energy it took me to compile and organize all the information that I would send out. There, of course, were the trips to the Post Office. I was on a first name basis with the postal employees. Total cost of marketing my son, not including labor, was approximately **$1400!**

Now you might say, "Well I wouldn't have to market my son or daughter to that many schools" and then send out only 10 packets. BIG MISTAKE!

The odds of finding the right school for your son or daughter by sending out only ten packets will be almost IMPOSSIBLE! Let alone finding the right school that will also offer an athletic scholarship or financial aid of any kind. The key to this approach is in numbers and sending packets to the right schools. In other words, finding the right school where your student-athlete can compete. If you haven't already, make sure you go right now to the first section in my book called "Evaluating your child's talent – A message to parents". Read this section thoroughly and listen to the message I'm trying to deliver.

If your child has the same Division I athletic potential that my son had, then consider sending packets out to between 50 and 100 schools to be safe (approximate cost - $2000). Start with the schools that are sending letters first. If your child has Division II potential, then you need to send out 200-300 packets (approximate cost - $2,000-$3,000). Yes, this can be very costly but nothing compared to the cost of a college education.

Creating Your Athlete Recruiting Profile

If you choose Option #2 the first place to start is to develop an "Athletic Recruiting Profile". Your profile should consist of the following items:

- A Cover Letter
- A Student Information Sheet

- A Highlight / Skills DVD
- Newspaper Articles

On the following pages we have included samples of some of the documents that should accompany your package. Specifically, there is a cover letter and a template for your biographical information, and information should you desire Dynamite Sports to make your athlete recruiting profile.

Sample Cover Letter

This letter should be written by the PARENT. I believe it is very important for the parent to make the initial contact with the college coach. This will send a clear message that you intend on being an important piece of your child's recruiting puzzle.

Dear Coach (coach's last name),

My name is (first & last name) and my (son/daughter), (athlete's name), has expressed interest in your university. I am enclosing some academic, athletic, and personal information about (him/her) along with a highlight DVD for you to review. *I realize that due to NCAA regulations you are not permitted to contact us yet, so* I will call you in about ten (10) days to make sure you received this material. Also, at that time, maybe you could answer a few questions we have about your university and your athletic program.

Sincerely,

————————————————

(parent's name)

If it is later than September 1st of your son or daughter's junior year in high school when you send this letter, you can delete that part of the letter that is in italics. After September 1st of their junior year, colleges are permitted to send high school athletes correspondence by mail.

Student-Athlete Information Sheet

This information sheet is similar to the ones that colleges send to prospective student-athletes in order to get background information on them. Take your time and answer all the information as accurately as possible.

You may want to also include two additional sections: a section covering the statistical data you have accumulated, and a section acknowledging the awards or honors that you have received.

STUDENT-ATHLETE INFORMATION SHEET

(Download actual form at www.dynamitesports.com)

PERSONAL

Full Name _____

Address _____

City, State, Zip _____

Home Phone _____ Mobile Phone _____

Email _____

Date of Birth _____ Social Sec. # _____

Birth City & St. _____

Height _____ Weight _____

Lives With (circle)   Mother   Father   Both   Guardian   Other

Mother's Name _____

Mother's Occupation _____

Mother's College _____

Mother's Employer _____

Mother's Work Phone _____

Father's Name _____

Father's Occupation _____

Father's College _____

Father's Employer _____

Father's Work Phone _____

Guardian's Name _____

Guardian's Work Phone _____

ACADEMIC

High School Name _____

Address _____

City, State, Zip _____

School Phone _____

GPA _____ SAT-V _____ SAT-M _____ ACT _____ Class Rank _____

Colleges you are interested in: 1 _____

2 _____   3 _____

College Prep: Yes _____ No _____ Academic Counselor _____

Academic Honors: _____

Potential College Major: _____

ATHLETIC

Major Sport _____ Years Played ___ Varsity _____ JV ___ Club ___

Positions Played: _____

HS Coach _____ Coach Phone _____

Speed: 20 Yd _____ 40 YD ___ 60 Yd _____ 100m _____ Other _____

Bench _____ Squat _____ Clean & Jerk _____

Other Sports: _____

Athletic Honors: _____

Highlight / Skills DVD

I don't mean game film, I mean a real highlight DVD that a college coach can view in his/her office and use to evaluate you without having to find you among twenty other athletes. You will want the highlight DVD to verify your athletic ability and physical attributes. The highlight DVD is the most important tool you will have to show college coaches what you have to offer.

If a college coach is interested in you after viewing your highlight DVD, they will probably ask your high school coach to send additional game film of you. This is a great sign that they are genuinely interested in you.

Newspaper Articles

Start collecting any NEWSPAPER ARTICLES that mention you. If you've lost or misplaced any, you can go to your local library, look them up on a disk and print them out. Make copies of each article no matter how much is written about you. Then, take a yellow highlighter and mark any part of the articles that specifically talks about you. We do this so the college coach won't have to read through an entire half page article just to find three sentences about you. Remember, we're consolidating the college coach's time.

Putting it all together

After you've gathered all this information, take the STUDENT-ATHLETE INFORMATION SHEET, your HIGHLIGHT DVD, and the copies of NEWSPAPER ARTICLES, put them in a flat rate priority mail envelope you can get at the post office. Attach a cover letter, similar to the one in this book, and send one to each of the colleges that are sending you letters. If you're not receiving any letters yet, pick out the colleges you are interested in and send one to each. You've just substantially increased your odds of getting a college athletic scholarship.

Selecting the Right Institution

After you've evaluated your talent and decided what level of college athletics would best suit you, it's time to start sending out marketing packets or your Athletic Recruiting Profile and looking at schools. Ask yourself general questions like:

1. Do I want to attend a small or large school?

2. Do I want to go far away or stay close to home?

3. Would I like the college to be in the city or country?

4. What major would I like to take?

5. What colleges offer my sport?

6. If my goal is to play as a freshman, will I have that opportunity?

I've compiled a list of all the institutions that offer intercollegiate athletics in the Appendix section of this handbook. We've broken them down by their division and state to make this process a little easier for you. While looking for schools, keep in mind that colleges can be Division I in one sport and Division II in others. It's really up to each university. You can check out each college individually by going to www.clas.ufl.edu/clas/american-universities.html. Click on the first letter of the college you want to find. Then a scrolling list will appear of every college or university in the country that begins with that letter. Scroll down the list until you find the school. After you click on the school, it will take you directly to that college's website. From there you can gather lots of useful information not only about their athletic programs, but also about their academics. You can also go to www.ncaa.org and search your sport to find out what division each school participates in. There are also several internet search engines that can pinpoint the colleges which meet your criteria. Some of these charge a fee, but a free one is www.collegesearch.net.

Remember, now is the time to start marketing yourself and gathering information about the school you are most interested in. **DON'T WASTE ANY TIME!** If you are a freshman or sophomore, start today. This will allow you time to prepare and find the right school for you. If you are a junior or senior, start yesterday!

Option #3 - You can get help from a professional

As you can see, Option #2 is not for everyone. It takes an ENORMOUS amount of time and effort and it may cost thousands of dollars $$$$$$ to do it properly. Maybe you just want to make sure you don't make any mistakes along the way or leave any stones unturned. After all, you just want to provide your son or daughter with the most quality opportunities possible! Right?

That brings us to Option #3. Yes, we are talking about using a professional in this field. Someone, or some company that has the skill, experience, resources, patience, reputation, and contacts, to do all of the above for a fair and reasonable cost to you the parent. We are talking about a "Recruiting Service or College Scouting Service".

I've added a section in my book about these services because I knew that families all across the country were being contacted by them. I thought it was important to educate parents so you understood what each type of service could offer.

First let me say this:

There isn't a book written (this one included), a speaker, a video produced, or any recruiting service that can take an average student and an average athlete and get them athletic scholarship money anywhere! IT'S JUST NOT GOING TO HAPPEN!

Hopefully, you're either a REALLY good student, and an EXCELLENT athlete, or a REALLY good athlete, and an EXCELLENT student, or somewhere in between. If you are, I can say with confidence, that there is a college or university somewhere out there that would love to have your son or daughter come to their school and participate in their athletic program. And, they would probably be willing to give them some sort of scholarship or financial aid too! The key is you finding them or them finding you.

After being approached by hundreds of parents across the country, asking me to recommend a service, I decided to go on a "fact finding mission." I needed to find out if there were any companies out there that were reputable and reasonable with respect to their efforts and costs. I contacted several companies under an alias of a parent of a freshman golfer in high school that was trying to decide whether to use a service like theirs or not. The information I obtained was FRIGHTENING! Even though I told them my son had a 1.9 GPA and probably wouldn't make the varsity squad until his senior year (get the picture), four of the companies were eager to talk to me and were very interested in taking my money up front. I hung up on them. The next three I spoke with seemed to be a little more realistic. But all they wanted to do was make a profile of my son and promised to "mail it" to as many as 1000 schools all over the country for a "substantial fee". All this without regard to what type of degree my son would be interested in, or what part of the country he wanted to attend college. I ended those conversations as well.

Then, I came across one company that threw me back, NCSA (Next College Student Athlete). On the surface they seemed to be somewhat unbelievable. When I contacted one of their regional scouts and gave him the same scenario about my fictitious son, the golfer, the first thing he told me was that my son may not QUALIFY for them to work with us. What! My son isn't good enough for your company to work with us? He explained that NCSA has academic and athletic requirements a student-athlete must meet in order to QUALIFY to use their services. WOW! That was the first indication that this company had high standards and stressed education first.

As it turned out, their academic requirements were similar to those of the NCAA. What a great idea! After a half-hour conversation we said our good-byes, and I sat there dumbfounded. I couldn't believe there was a recruiting service out there that wouldn't take anyone's money regardless of the situation. I searched through their website after the phone call to check them out some more.

Then I called their corporate office and asked for some references of families they had worked with three years ago and some family references they were working with right now. They honored my request as though they had nothing to hide, but I knew better (so I thought). After contacting seven families, and talking with several moms and dads at length about the services NCSA provided, I was sold! Every parent I spoke with had nothing but kind things to say. Of course, some were more pleased than others. But when I asked each family if they could do it all over again, would they still use NCSA, they all said the same thing. YES!

Now, what do some of these services charge? Well, the eight that I looked at ranged in price from $600 to $4000! Yes, that's a lot of money. But then again, so is the cost of a college education. If you consider using a college scouting service, I would say this: If spending $1500 for a service is going to keep food off the table or keep you from making your mortgage payment, you simply don't do it. You can use "option #2", do it yourself, and control the amount of money you spend sending out packets keeping in mind the more you send out, the more chance of success you will have. Here are some important guidelines to use when looking at a service:

- Make sure they charge a one-time, up-front fee and not a commission based on what scholarship money they get your child. (This would be an NCAA violation and deem your child ineligible to play in college)
- Ask if they can sort or filter your child's profile to only those types of colleges you are interested in. (ie: small school, warm climate, teaching degree, etc.)
- Make sure that they will represent you until you graduate college. So many athletes choose a school for the wrong reasons and end up transferring to another institution. If they are there to help you with this situation without any additional cost your transition will go much quicker.
- Insist on an unconditional money back guarantee that if you are unsatisfied for any reason whatsoever they will refund your money.

The bottom line is this. If you don't do anything, you will wonder what happened after it is too late, or you will wonder why you didn't get the offers that you had hoped for.

How to Use Social Media for Recruiting
– Content provided by NCSA

Whenever social media and college athletic recruiting pop up in the news, the articles usually focus on recruits who have lost an offer or a scholarship because of their poor social media choices. However, social media when used properly, can be an effective recruiting tool. In fact, recruits can use the power of social media to contact coaches, show coaches what kind of recruit they are and even gain the attention of college coaches who weren't previously recruiting them.

NCAA rules on social media in recruiting

The NCAA rules about social media in recruiting can be a little confusing. DI and DII coaches can direct message recruits starting either June 15 or September 1 of their junior year of high school, depending on the sport. At this time, coaches are also able to "like," "share," "retweet" or "favorite" a recruit's posts. Here's where it gets a little tricky. Coaches are not allowed to publicly communicate with recruits until after the athletes has committed to their program. This means that they are not allowed to post on a recruit's Facebook wall or Twitter feed until after they've committed to the school.

This is often referred to as the "click don't type rule," which helps coaches remember that they can interact with recruits' social media but they can't actually type anything to them on their public profiles. As a recruit, you don't need to worry about these rules, but it's important to know what to type of communication to expect from college coaches.

How college coaches use social media in recruiting

Coaches have begun to embrace social media in recruiting to help them accomplish a few key goals. Depending on the size of the program and the resources, coaches will have interns and/or recruiting coordinators scour Twitter to see which athletes have gotten offers from rival schools or similar programs. Coaches don't want to lose a top recruit—especially to a rival school!

Insider tip: If you receive an offer from a school, you can attempt to capture the attention of other coaches by tweeting about it. Keep it simple—mention how grateful you are for the opportunity and be sure to tag the coach or athletic program you received the offer from. However, never, ever invent or inflate an offer just to get attention. Coaches will do their research on you, and they will find out eventually if your offer is not legit. This kind of behavior can eventually leave you with no offers.

The second key way coaches use social media in recruiting is to get a better understanding of a recruit's personality and character. In fact, 85 percent of college coaches surveyed by Cornerstone Reputation said their staff conducted online research of recruits. Of these coaches, 87 percent have turned to Facebook, 79 percent have used Twitter and 65 percent have looked at Instagram to gain insight into a recruit's character. While inappropriate content will not only deter coaches from recruiting you but also cause coaches to rescind offers, positive social media posts can make coaches even more interested in recruiting you.

These guidelines can help you create a strong, positive online social media presence that will impress college coaches.

Set all your accounts to public

While your first instinct might be to try and hide all your social media accounts from coaches, in fact, the opposite is true. Coaches know that most—if not all—recruits have at least one social media account and they will search for it. If they see your profile is restricted, they will assume that you have something to hide. To eliminate that uncertainty, make it easy for the coach to find you.

Insider tip: To go the extra mile in transparency, send your social media handles to coaches in your messages to them. This way, they can easily look you up—because they likely will anyway—and they know you have nothing to hide. An added bonus: The coach may start following you on Twitter to keep up with your progress.

"Follow" and "Like" athletic programs you're interested in

Keeping tabs on your favorite teams via social media is a great way to get alerted when the team wins, loses, gets an award or something else noteworthy takes place. These are all helpful conversation starters to use when you're emailing, texting or direct messaging a coach. Coaches want to know that you're genuinely interested in their school, and having insider knowledge about their program is a great way to show you've done your homework. You may even score a follow or like back from the coach!

Insider tip: Try following the program's strength and conditioning coaches, trainers and some current athletes, in addition to the head coach. Most recruits' will default to only following the head coach—which is a great—but you might get important information by following other staff members. They may post workouts you can try or give you insights into the athletes' day-to-day schedule.

Direct message coaches for quicker response times

While we can't guarantee coaches will respond to your direct messages, we have found that coaches tend to respond quicker to DMs than emails. Think about DMs as another tool in your belt to communicate with coaches—some may prefer to go through social media, while others prefer to connect through email, text or phone calls. Just like when sending an email to a college coach [link to page] keep your DM short and to the point. Open the message with something about the program and then give the coach a few key stats about yourself. Don't forget to link to your NCSA profile so the coach can view your information!

Insider tip: Update your Twitter account to receive DMs from people you aren't following. Finding and following every college coach on Twitter would be a full-time job! Depending on the phone you're using, either tap the gear icon in your "Me" tab, click on the navigation menu or click on your profile icon. Select "Settings" and tap "Privacy and content." Next to "Receive Direct Messages from anyone," either slide the twitch or check the box to enable the feature.

Show your sport IQ and—humbly—highlight your accomplishments

Your social media accounts are great places to post some of your favorite articles about your sport, share inspirational quotes and post your highlight videos. Call out academic or athletic awards you've received, positive feedback about a recent camp experience, college visits you've been on and firm offers from coaches. Avoid any inappropriate language, racial or sexist slurs, and anything overtly political. This rule also applies to your user name.

Don't allow other people to post inappropriate content on your social media accounts

Monitoring your social media accounts is going to be a key part of your recruiting process, because you may be dedicated to posting only positive content on your accounts, but your friends may not follow suit. You can use Facebook Timeline Review to check all posts and choose which ones appear on your wall.

To set up Facebook Timeline Review, log in to your Facebook account and click the down arrow at the top right corner of the tool bar (next to the lock symbol). On the dropdown menu, select "Settings." In the left-hand column, click "Timeline and Tagging" and look for "Review posts friends tag you in before they appear on your Timeline?" Click "Edit" and select "Enabled" from the dropdown menu

Part of the Reigning Champs Team

NCSA Athletic Recruiting

NCSA Athletic Recruiting, the official recruiting partner of Dynamite Sports, is part of the Reigning Champs network. NCSA believes in the transformational power of sport and is focused on empowering student-athletes to play at the next level. Since 2000, they have helped more than 80,000 student-athletes commit to the right college fit — and have placed student-athletes at more than 90 percent of U.S. colleges and universities.

Creating an NCSA account allows student-athletes and their families to take control of their recruiting. More than just a video or an online profile, every NCSA account includes a free recruiting consultation with an expert, where one of more than 500 former college athletes and coaches on the NCSA Athletic Recruiting team provide answers and advice specific to your family's particular situation and path-to-college preferences.

Through an NCSA account, student-athletes can search for roster openings and scholarship opportunities, learn how well they match with their favorite college programs (and find new opportunities they didn't know existed!) and connect directly with coaches through a central messaging center — no more tracking down college coaches' email addresses or contact information in different athletic department websites.

NCSA also provides comprehensive digital recruiting education, which families can access in group online workshops or at their own pace through NCSA University, a collection of customized activities, tools and a resource library, to help every family understand the recruiting process from the first moment your student-athlete chooses to play college athletics all the way through stepping on campus as a first-year college student.

RECRUITING

Well, here it is the part of the material you've all been waiting for. RECRUITING! You must understand that recruiting is a game played by professionals. College coaches are trying to sell you on their school. Depending on what grade you're in, you may or may not be getting letters from colleges yet. If you are receiving letters or contacts, create a folder for each college and place any correspondence they send you in it. It pays to be organized. Included in this book is a "College Information Sheet". Fill out one of these for each college that's contacting you. If you don't have all the information you need, call the university anytime you want. They'll be happy to answer all your questions. You can use these sheets to compare universities and what each has to offer. Ask your guidance counselor to gather information on each college you're interested in. Make sure they offer the curriculum you want to pursue most. After completing the sheet, put it in the folder for that university.

In the back of this handbook you'll find a glossary containing many key words used in the recruiting process. Read this section thoroughly. You need to be familiar with each of these terms in detail. Once you have an understanding of the terms, continue with the "General Recruiting Information." I've taken these important questions & answers out of the "Coaches Recruiting Guide." Read them all because they pertain to you, the student-athlete. I promise you that you'll learn a lot about recruiting and what the colleges are allowed to do and what you are allowed to do. Next, read the "Recruiting Guidelines" sheet. It will summarize a lot of the recruiting information and give you tips on how to make the most of the recruiting process.

Next, take a look at the "Recruiting Calendars" for your sport. This will give you an idea of what the different recruiting periods look like. As you can see, there are specific dates for everything. College coaches must adhere to these structured time frames, otherwise they will be in violation of NCAA rules and could expose you to possible ineligibility. Don't ever compromise what you know is right and what is wrong when it comes to recruiting. It's YOUR ELIGIBILTY, not theirs!

Now that I've given you a good background about recruiting, it's time to make a "PLAN." Start, by making a "Long List" of maybe 10-15 schools that you're interested in. Then, schedule two unofficial visits during your freshman year. Visit a D-1 and a D-3 school. Schedule additional visits during your next three years. Take your college information sheets with you to fill out on your visits. By doing this, you'll get an idea of what each college has to offer, what their program is like, and if you seem to fit there or not. You'll know whether it "feels right." You've just started the recruiting process on your own terms and at your own pace. If you can, make these unofficial visits a family event. After all, this will be a very special time in your life and it's only going to happen once. Enjoy it with people who love you and care about you. It will make the recruiting process very special.

As you make each visit, make it a point to meet with the Head Coach and assistant coaches. You also want to meet with the academic advisor for your sport. Have them show you what's required academically of an athlete at their school and find out if they specialize in any of the programs you may want to major in. Check out all their facilities from the weight room to the practice facilities and stadium, to the locker rooms and training room. By visiting their school, you're showing them that you are genuinely interested. They like that!

During the recruiting process, you may get phone calls from college coaches. This is a great time to acquire more information about each college. Use your College Information Sheets. If you're not interested in a particular school, politely tell the coach when they call. This will save both of you time and will allow them to concentrate their efforts on recruiting someone else that is more interested in their school.

Another way to get a feel for a school would be to go to a sporting event there. Colleges are permitted to give you up to three free tickets to home sporting events, and you don't have to wait to be invited. Call and tell them you'd like to come see a sporting event at their university to get a better look at their facilities. Trust me, they'll bend over backwards to get you there.

After you've taken all the unofficial visits you want, take your "long list" of schools and sit down with your parents and evaluate all the schools. Use your "College Information Sheets" to help remember what each one had to offer. Which ones had the better facilities, which had the best academic programs, etc? Then, narrow your schools down to a "short list" of five. At this point, if it is during your senior year of high school you may ask the five schools for an official visit, if they haven't already offered one, or you can use all the information you've gathered to make your decision now. Know all your options, who is offering you a FULL SCHOLARSHIP and who is offering a PARTIAL SCHOLARSHIP.

Sit down with your parents and discuss all your options - the pro's and con's of each university. Ask for their input because they will have a different perspective than you. Then, the final decision will be yours. It's your life and this decision will shape your future. But don't worry; after all the preparation, you're ready to make this decision. Good luck and God bless you.

Creating a Recruiting Plan

Gathering College Information

Hopefully you receive letters or information back from the colleges that you sent your recruiting packets to. Take your list and combine it with the list of colleges that have sent you letters. Fill out as much information on the **College Information Sheet** that you can. Check out each college's website; if you don't know the URL use an internet search engine. You will probably need to call the college to get some of the information. Phone numbers can be found on college websites, or your school library or guidance counselor may have a book called The National Directory of College Athletics.

This is a good resource tool because it lists all of the coaches at every college including their phone number and address. There are two books, one for men's sports and the other for women's sports. This book can also be found online at www.collegiatedirectories.com.

Contact College Coaches

Don't be afraid to contact college coaches to let them know you're interested. Phone calls and email generated by you is allowed at any time, but you can also chat or instant message them. Ask them information about their programs and let them know of any evaluation events that you are planning to attend. Be proactive and persistent, your phone calls or emails may be the factor that gets you financial aid.

COLLEGE INFORMATION SHEET

(Download actual form at www.dynamitesports.com)

College _____

Address _____

City, State, Zip _____

School Phone _____ Athletic Phone _____

Enrollment (U) _____ Enrollment (G) _____

Head Coach _____ Position Coach _____

Recruiting Coach _____ Recruiting Secretary _____

Strength Coach _____ Academic Counselor _____

Position Recruited for: _____ Depth Chart Projection _____

Number of Recruits for Position: ____ Redshirt Prospects: _____

Scholarship Offered   Yes _____   No _____

Other Costs   Yes _____   No _____ $ _____

Official Visit Offered   Yes _____   No _____   Visit Date _____

Athletic Graduation Rate _____ Sport Graduation Rate _____

SAT/ACT Score Required _____ Avg Team Score _____

Counselors Available _____ Study Hall Required _____

Conference _____ Conference Finish _____

Post Season _____

Schedule _____

Season Tickets Available Yes _____ No_____ Quantity _____ Cost _____

Rating (5 is best)	1	2	3	4	5
Head Coach	1	2	3	4	5
Position Coach	1	2	3	4	5
Recruiting Coach	1	2	3	4	5
Strength Coach	1	2	3	4	5
Players	1	2	3	4	5
Team Chemistry	1	2	3	4	5
Academic Counselor	1	2	3	4	5
Academic Support	1	2	3	4	5
Locker Room	1	2	3	4	5
Training Facilities	1	2	3	4	5
Playing Facilities	1	2	3	4	5
Housing / Lodging	1	2	3	4	5
Campus	1	2	3	4	5
Area	1	2	3	4	5

Notes: _____

_____

_____

_____

Take Unofficial Visits

Many student-athletes choose the wrong level of college. Then they find themselves sitting the bench for two or three years or maybe never stepping onto the playing field or court. The NCAA has a staggering statistic. They told us that 26% of all incoming scholarship freshman athletes end up leaving college before the end of their first year! One way to help make the right college choice is to take several unofficial visits to different size schools. What is an unofficial visit? It is a visit to a college or university that you pay for, not the college. I recommend you take unofficial visits to at least one D-I school and one D- III school your freshman year. This will allow you to get a look at different size athletic programs and help you find your **"COMFORT LEVEL"**. Your guidance counselor or high school coach can help you pick which colleges to visit. It is extremely important that you take these visits as early as 9th grade. It will allow you time to decide what level of colleges to focus on, show you where you will fit the best and where you can play. Then, you will have three or four years to prepare for college athletics.

How do you go about setting up these unofficial visits? IT'S EASY! All you need to do is call the college you would like to visit and ask for the athletic office of the sport that you are in. Then ask to speak to the recruiting coordinator or recruiting coach for your area. Tell them you would like to visit their school and get a better look at their athletic facilities and their academic programs. Trust me, they will bend over backwards to get you there. Remember, for all they know you could be the next superstar that will help their program WIN! After you agree on an appropriate date for your visit, give the coach a list of things you would like to see and do while you are there. Below is a list of items to include:

- Meet with the head coach
- Meet with your position coach
- Meet with the academic advisor for your sport
- Visit their playing and practice facilities and weight room
- Visit the head trainer and physical therapy area
- Look at a typical dorm

You should also meet an athlete on the team, but don't tell the coach about this request prior to your arrival. You don't want them to "hand pick" someone for you to meet. Wait until you are there, then YOU pick an athlete to talk to. This will allow you to get an unrehearsed account of what the athletic program is like and how the athletes feel about the coaching staff. Below, I've listed some questions you may want to ask.

1. Start by asking their hometown and high school size.
2. Then ask how they fit at this university.
3. If they could do it all over again, would they still come here?
4. Has the coaching staff delivered on things they said would happen once they came here?
5. Ask them to rate the coaching staff.

6. What is the training regimen like?

7. Does the academic support staff actively work with the athletes?

8. How often are they able to get home?

9. Do they encourage parents to visit the campus?

Ask the athlete any other questions you feel are relevant and then thank them for being helpful.

Take your **"College Information Sheets"** with you on these visits and fill them out. Answer all the questions and be sure to rate all the facilities and coaches you meet. This will be a great help to you later when you try to evaluate and compare each university and athletic program. By the time you leave, you will know if you would fit in there or not. Plan your next unofficial visit and follow the same plan as you did for the first. After you have made as many unofficial visits as possible, sit down with your parents and / or coach and evaluate each university. Using your college information sheets as a guideline complete the **"College Comparison Worksheet"**. By taking unofficial visits and using these tools, you will be more prepared and better able to decide what direction you want to go and what schools you want to pursue.

College Comparison

Use the table below to help you rate colleges according to the factors you feel are important. List the items which are important in the left-most column and place the visited colleges in the top row. Using a scale of 1 -10, where 1 is poor and 10 is excellent, rate each college by your important factors. Total each column to determine which college ranks the highest according to the factors.

Important Factors	College 1	College 2	College 3	College 4	College 5
1.					
2.					
3.					
4.					
5.					
6.					
7.					
8.					
9.					
10.					
Total					

General Recruiting Information

Recruiting Frequently Asked Questions

Q: When are prospects eligible for recruiting contact?

High school prospects may be contacted during permissible contact periods on or after July 1, after completion of their junior year. Exception: Members of the athletics staffs at U.S. Air Force, Military, and Naval Academies may contact prospects who are in their junior year.

Q: When may institutions send recruiting materials to prospects?

D-I and D-II colleges may send prospects camp brochures and questionnaires as early as ninth grade. Recruiting materials for most sports may be sent on or after September 1 of the prospect's junior year in high school. Exceptions: Men's Basketball can send materials after June 15th at the end of the sophomore year

Q: What recruiting materials may they provide to you or your coach?

General correspondence, faxes or e-mail, newspaper clippings, pre-enrollment information, game programs, one annual athletics publication, official academic, admissions and student-services publications, schedule cards, and student-athlete handbooks.

Q: What is the difference between official and unofficial visits?

Prospects' official visits are paid for by an institution; unofficial visits are paid for by the individual prospects. If an institution pays for any of a prospect's expenses or provides entertainment other than activities expressly permitted by NCAA regulations, the prospect's visit becomes official.

Q: When may prospects make unofficial visits?

Prospects may take unofficial visits at any time. Exception: There can be no unofficial visits for Men's Basketball during the month of July.

Q: How many times may a prospect visit a campus?

A prospect may take an unlimited number of unofficial visits. A high school senior may take a maximum of five (5) official visits to NCAA institutions (with no more than one permitted to any one institution). Official Visits may not last longer than 48 hours.

Q: What, if any, transportation may an institution provide on an official visit?

An institution may provide round trip transportation for the prospect. They may provide car-mileage reimbursement, to the individual incurring the expenses (except for the prospect's coach), or they may pay for bus or train fare, coach air fare for commercial flights, or air fare at established charter rates for noncommercial flights.

Q: In what instances may an institution provide meals and lodging?

In Division I, on an official visit, an institution may provide meals and lodging to a prospect and the prospect's parents or spouse. Additional persons (e.g., prospect's brother, sister, friend) may stay in the same room as the prospect, but the institution may not pay costs resulting from additional occupants, and any additional occupants may not be prospects being recruited by that institution.

Q: How many off-campus contacts are allowed?

In most sports institutions may contact a prospect no more than three times at any off-campus site (regardless of the number of sports in which the prospect is being recruited). Any in-person, off-campus contact made with a prospect regarding the signing of a letter of intent or other commitment to attend an institution is prohibited

However

- In Division I basketball, they are limited to seven recruiting opportunities of which not more than three may be contacts.

- In Division I ice hockey, they are limited to seven recruiting opportunities (contacts & evaluations) per prospect, of which not more than three may be contacts.

- In Divisions I-A & I-AA football, seven in-person contacts per prospect are permitted during the contact period either at the prospect's educational institution or any other location. Not more than one contact is permitted in any calendar week (Sunday through Saturday). In Division I-A football, the head coach may make in-person, off-campus contact with a prospect (or the prospect's parents or legal guardians) only during one calendar day. Assistants can accompany the head coach during those contacts, as long as they still comply with other regulations that normally apply to them.

Q: Where may prospects be contacted and evaluated?

Prospects may be visited or evaluated at their homes, schools, or other off-campus sites, as well as on an institution's campus. There are guidelines for contacts or evaluations at each site.

- In Division I football, an institution can visit a prospect's school no more than once a week during a contact period, regardless of whether the visit is for contact or evaluation purposes or if there is more than one prospect that is being recruited at a particular school.

- Visiting a prospect's school on consecutive days to observe a tournament or tier of a tournament counts as a single visit.

- Prospects may not be contacted before any athletics competition at any site on the days that the prospects are participants.

- In Divisions I-A and I-AA football, coaches may visit a prospect's school on one day, and only for evaluation purposes, during the October - November evaluation period. Off-campus contacts may not be made prior to the first football contact period following the prospect's completion of the junior year in high school.

- In Division I basketball, coaches may visit a prospect's school on one day, and only for evaluation purposes, during an evaluation period. In men's basketball no off-campus contact can occur with a prospect until after September 9 of their senior year.

Q: May prospects be contacted during the signing period for the National Letter of Intent?

The National Letter of Intent is a standard form used by many Divisions I and II institutions, and it has an initial date for prospects to sign their letters. In all Division I sports, this date is surrounded by a four-day dead period, when no on-or-off-campus contacts or evaluations of prospects can occur.

In Division II sports, a 48-hour dead period precedes the initial signing date. During the dead period, the letter must be mailed to the prospect; it may not be hand-delivered. The letter may be delivered by express mail, courier service, regular mail or facsimile machine. Any in-person, off-campus contact made with a prospect for the purpose of signing a letter of intent or attendance at activities related to the signing of a letter of intent or other commitment to attend an institution is prohibited.

Q: When may prospects in sports other than football and basketball not be contacted and evaluated?

During the National Letter of Intent dead periods and the following sports specific dates:

- Division I Field hockey - Wednesday before the NCAA championship game to noon on the day after the game.

- Division I Women's Gymnastics - Wednesday before the NCAA championships to Sunday (noon) after the championships.

- Division I Men's Ice hockey - Wednesday before the NCAA championship to Sunday (noon) after the championship.

- Division I Softball - Tuesday before the NCAA championship game to noon on the day after the game and the period 12:01 a.m. on the day of registration for the national convention of the National Softball Coaches Assoc. to 12:01 a.m. on the day after adjournment of the convention.

- Division I Women's Volleyball - Wednesday before the NCAA championship game through December 31.

Q: When and how may prospects be contacted or evaluated after they have signed the National Letter of Intent?

After the calendar day on which a prospect has signed a Letter of Intent to attend an institution (or, for institutions not subscribing to the National Letter of Intent, the calendar day after the prospect's signed acceptance of the institution's written offer of admission and/or financial aid), there are no limits on the number of contacts you may have with the prospect (or the prospect's relatives or legal guardians) or evaluations of the prospect. However there are guidelines.

Q: When may prospects be contacted by telephone?

In Divisions I and II sports other than football, or basketball, college staff such as faculty members and coaches may not make telephone calls to prospects (or the prospect's parents or legal guardians) until July 1st (D-I), or June 15th (D-II) after prospects have completed their junior year in high school. Institutions are permitted to make only one call per week to each prospect (or their parents or legal guardians).

- In Division I-A Football, one telephone call to a prospect may be made during the month of May of the prospect's junior year in high school. Additional calls to a prospect may not be made before September 1 of the beginning of the prospect's senior year in high school. Thereafter, telephone contact with a prospect is limited to once per week outside the contact period. During a contact period, telephone contact may be made with a senior prospect at the institution's discretion.

- In Divisions I-AA and II Football, colleges may not telephone a prospect before September 1 after completion of the prospect's junior year in high school. Thereafter, telephone contact with a prospect is limited to once per week outside the contact period. During a contact period, telephone contact may be made with a senior prospect at the institution's discretion.

- In Division I Men's basketball, it is permissible to make one telephone call per month beginning June 15 before the prospect's junior year through July 31. Then institutions are allowed to phone twice a week beginning August 1 of the prospect's senior year.

- In Division I Women's basketball, it is permissible to make one telephone per month in April, May and from June 1 to June 20 of the prospect's junior year. Then one call may be made between June 21 and June 30, and three times in July after the prospect's junior year. Then institutions are allowed to phone once a week beginning August 1 of the prospect's senior year.

- In Division I Ice hockey, it is permissible to make one telephone call to a prospect who is a resident of a foreign country during the month of July after completion of the prospect's sophomore year in high school.

- There are exceptions to the one-call-a-week limit. You may make an unrestricted number of calls to a prospect (or the prospect's parents or legal guardians) under the following circumstances:

- During the five days immediately before the prospect's official visit to an institution;

- On the day of an institution's permissible off-campus contact with the prospect; and

- On the initial signing date for the fall or spring National Letter of Intent and for the two days after that signing date. In Division I football, unlimited telephone calls are permitted two days before and two days after the initial signing date for the National Letter of Intent.

- After the calendar day on which the prospect signs a National Letter of Intent with an institution.

Q: When and how may financial aid (scholarships) be offered to prospects?

During the recruiting process, it is permissible to make scholarship offers to prospects-that is, grant-in-aid to attend an institution. The following items are examples of PROHIBITED financial offers:

- Cash

- Employment arrangements for a prospect's relatives

- Co-signing of loans

- Loans to a prospect's friends or relatives

Q: What benefits may an institution offer to prospects?

An institution can offer several types of benefits to prospects, in addition to financial aid. These benefits include job arrangements, assistance in obtaining educational loans, summer housing, admission to athletics events and alumni events.

- Job arrangements. An institution may arrange for a prospect's employment. The prospect may not begin the job until after the completion of the prospect's senior year in high school.

- Complimentary admissions to athletic events. An institution may provide free admissions to campus athletics events to prospects visiting their campus. On official visits, the prospect's parents (or legal guardians) or spouses also may receive free admissions to campus athletics events. On unofficial visits, they may provide a maximum of three complimentary admissions for prospects and the individuals who accompany them, such as parents or friends. In Division I during the conduct of the event (including intermission) prospects and the other guests must be seated in the general seating section and not in special boxes, press areas or the team's bench area.

- Summer housing. Prospects may rent dormitory space from an institution over the summer. These arrangements must be part of that institution's regular policy and be available to all prospective students.

Q: How may signings be announced?

Prospects, or their families, may arrange press conferences to announce their decisions regarding enrollment. They must act independently; the institution and its boosters may not be involved.

Divisional Recruiting Guidelines

Division I

In addition to general recruiting regulations, no alumni, boosters or representatives of a college's athletics interests may be involved in your recruiting. There may be no phone calls or letters from boosters.

The restriction doesn't apply to recruiting by alumni or representatives as part of a college's regular admissions program for all prospective students, including non-athletes.

You (or your family) may not receive any benefit, inducement or arrangement such as cash, clothing, cars, improper expenses, transportation, gifts or loans to encourage you to sign a National Letter of Intent or attend an NCAA college.

Letters from coaches, faculty members and students (but not boosters) aren't permitted until September 1 at the beginning of your junior year.

Telephone Calls

In all sports other than football and basketball, telephone calls to a prospective student-athlete [or the prospective student-athlete's relatives or legal guardian(s)] may not be made before July 1 following the completion of the prospective student-athlete's junior year in high school, thereafter, staff members shall not make such telephone calls more than once a week.

In Division I-A an I-AA football, an institution's coaches may telephone a prospect once between April 15 and May 31 of the prospect's junior year in high school. Additional telephone calls to a prospect [or a prospect's relatives or legal guardians(s)] may not be made before September 1 of the beginning of the prospect's senior year in high school , thereafter, such telephone contact is limited to once a week outside of a contact period. Also, an institution's football coaches may telephone you as often as they wish during the period 48 hours before and 48 hours after 7 a.m. on the initial signing date for the National Letter of Intent.

In Division I men's basketball, an institution is permitted to make one telephone call per month to a prospect [or the prospect's parents or legal guardian(s)] on or after June 15 of the prospect's sophomore year in high school through July 31 of the prospect's junior year in high school. Further, an institution is permitted to make two telephone calls per week to a prospect [or the prospect's parents or legal guardian(s)] beginning August 1 prior to the prospect's senior year in high school. An institution is permitted to make one telephone call per week to a two-year college prospect [or the prospect's parents or legal guardian(s)].

In Division I women's basketball, one telephone call to a prospect [or the prospect's parents or legal guardian(s)] may be made during each of the months of April and May of the prospect's junior year in high school. One call may be made on or after June 1 and June 20 and one call may be made on or after June 21 through June 30 of the prospect's junior year in high school. In addition, only three telephone calls to a prospect [or the prospect's parents or legal guardian(s)] may be made during the month of July following the prospect's junior year in high school, with no more than one telephone call per week. Thereafter, staff members shall not make such telephone calls more than once per week.

In Division I ice hockey, an institution's coaches may telephone a prospect who is a resident of a foreign country once during the month of July following the completion of the prospect's sophomore year in high school.

Exceptions to the one call per week regulation may be made under the following circumstances:

- During the five days immediately before your official visit by the college you will be visiting;
- On the day of a coach's off-campus contact with you by that coach; and
- On the initial date for signing the National Letter of Intent in your sport through two days after the initial signing date.

You (or your parents) may telephone a coach at your expense as often as you wish.

Coaches also may accept collect calls from you and may use a toll-free (800, 877, or 888) number to receive telephone calls from you on or after July 1 after completion of your junior year.

Enrolled student-athletes may not make recruiting telephone calls to you. Enrolled students (non-athletes) may telephone you as part of a college's regular admissions program directed at all prospective students. Enrolled students (including student-athletes) may receive telephone calls at your expense on or after July 1 after completion of your junior year.

Contacts

In all sports except football and men's basketball, a college coach may contact a prospect in person once in April at the prospect's high school. Any additional contact cannot occur again until July 1 after completion of the junior year. Any face-to-face meeting between a college coach and you or your parents, during which any of you say more than "hello" may be considered a contact. Also, any face-to-face meeting that is prearranged or that occurs at your high school or competition or practice site is a contact, regardless of the conversation. These contacts are not permissible "bumps."

Currently in all sports other than football and women's basketball, coaches have seven recruiting opportunities (contacts and evaluations) during the academic year and not more than three of the seven opportunities may be in-person, off-campus contacts. A college coach may visit your high school (with the approval of your high-school principal) only once a week during a contact period.

Football coaches may contact you off the college campus six times. However, no more than one contact per week may occur during a contact period, regardless of where the contact occurs. Off-campus contacts may not be made prior to the first football contact period following the prospect's completion of the junior year in high school.

In men's basketball, during the academic year, each institution shall be limited to seven recruiting opportunities (contacts and evaluations combined) per prospective student-athlete but may not include more than three in-person, off-campus contacts which may be made after September 9 of the prospective student-athlete's senior year

In women's basketball, during the academic year, each institution shall be limited to five recruiting opportunities (contacts and evaluations combined) per prospective student-athlete but may not include more than three in-person, off-campus contacts which may be made after September 16 of the prospective student-athlete's senior year.

In women's gymnastics, additional off-campus contacts may not be made until July 15 after the completion of the prospect's junior year.

Evaluations

An evaluation is any off-campus activity used to assess your academic qualifications or athletics ability, including a visit to your high school (during which no contact occurs) or watching you practice or compete at any site.

Currently in all sports other than football and basketball, institutions have seven permissible recruiting opportunities (contacts and evaluations) during the academic year, and not more than three of the seven opportunities may be in-person, off-campus contacts.

In football, institutional staff members shall be limited to three evaluations during the academic year during which the prospective student-athlete competes or practices on any team. Not more than one evaluation may be used during the fall evaluation period and not more than two evaluations may be used during the April 15 through May 31 evaluation period. An authorized off-campus recruiter may use one evaluation to assess the prospective student-athlete's athletics ability and one evaluation to assess the prospective student-athlete's academic qualifications during the April 15 through May 31 evaluation period. If an institution's coaching staff member conducts both an athletics and an academic evaluation of a prospective student-athlete on the same day during the April 15 through May 31 evaluation period, the institution shall be charged with the use of an academic evaluation only and shall be permitted to conduct a second athletics evaluation of the prospective student-athlete on a separate day during the April 15 through the May 31 evaluation period.

In women's basketball, during the academic year, each institution shall be limited to five recruiting opportunities (contacts and evaluations combined) per prospective student-athlete, and not more than three of the five opportunities may be contacts. Women's basketball staff members shall not exceed 85 person days during the academic year.

All contacts and evaluations must adhere to the recruiting calendar established for each particular sport. A coach may only contact you off the college campus and/or attend your practices and games to evaluate your athletics ability during a designated contact or evaluation period.

Consult the recruiting calendars to determine when contacts and evaluations are permissible for your sport.

Official Visits

With the exception of men's basketball, Official visits are offered after a prospect starts their senior year. Men's basketball can offer an official visit after January 1 of the prospect's junior year.

Prospects may only have one expense-paid (official) visit to a particular campus and may receive no more than five such visits. This restriction applies even if you are being recruited in more than one sport.

Before you can receive an official visit, the college must have on their premises an academic transcript and a score from a PSAT, an SAT, a PACT Plus or an ACT taken on a national test date under national testing conditions. Your academic transcript may be a photocopy of your official high-school (or college) transcript. {Note: In this instance, the Division I school may use the services of the NCAA Eligibility Center to validate your credentials.]

During your official visit (which may not exceed 48 hours), you may receive round-trip transportation between your home (or high school) and the campus, and you (and your parents) may receive meals, lodging and complimentary admissions to campus athletics events. A coach may only accompany you on your official visit when the transportation occurs by automobile and all transportation occurs within the 48-hour period. Meals provided to you (and/or your parents) on an official visit may be provided either on or off the institution's campus.

The complimentary admissions you receive may provide you seating only in the facility's general seating area. You may not be given special seating (e.g., press box, bench area).

A student host may help you (and your family) become acquainted with campus life. The host may spend $30 per day to cover all costs of entertaining you (and your parents, legal guardians or spouse); however, the money can't be used to purchase souvenirs such as T-shirts or other college mementos. Additionally, during a campus visit, the school may provide you with a student-athlete handbook.

Printed Materials

A Division I college that is recruiting you may provide to you only the following printed materials on or after September 1 of your junior year:

- Official academic, admissions and student services publications and videotapes published by the college;
- General correspondence, including letters and college note cards (attachments to correspondence may include materials printed on plain white paper with black ink);
- Game programs (a college may only give you a program on an official or unofficial visit; colleges may not mail you a program);
- A media guide or recruiting brochure (but not both) in each sport;
- Any necessary pre-enrollment information about orientation, conditioning, academics, practice activities, as long as you have signed a National Letter of Intent or have been accepted for enrollment;
- One student-athlete handbook. (A college may only give you a handbook on an official or unofficial visit. A college may mail you a handbook once you've signed a National Letter of Intent or been accepted for enrollment.)
- One wallet-size playing schedule card in each sport.
- A Division I college may show you a highlight film/videotape, but may not send it to or leave it with you or your coach.
- A Division I college also may provide you a questionnaire, camp brochure and educational information published by the NCAA (such as this guide) at any time.

Division II

In addition to general recruiting regulations, no alumni or representatives of a college's athletics interests (boosters or representatives) may be involved in off-campus recruiting; however, you may receive letters from boosters, faculty members, students and coaches on or after September 1 of your junior year.

You (or your family) may not receive any benefit, inducement or arrangement such as cash, clothing, cars, improper expenses, transportation, gifts or loans to encourage you to sign an institutional or conference letter of intent or to attend an NCAA school.

Telephone Calls

In all sports, telephone calls from coaches and faculty members are permissible on or after June 15 before your senior year.

After this, a college coach or faculty member is limited to one telephone call per week to you (or your parents or legal guardians), except that unlimited calls to you (or your parents or legal guardians) may be made under the following circumstances:

- During the five days immediately before your official visit (by the college you'll be visiting);
- On the day of the coach's off-campus contact with you; and
- On the initial date for signing the National Letter of Intent in your sport through the two days after the initial signing date.

In Division II football, however, unlimited phone calls to you may be made during a contact period and once a week outside of a contact period.

Coaches may accept collect calls and use a toll-free (1.800, 1.877, or 1.888) number to receive telephone calls from you (or your parents or legal guardians) at any time.

Enrolled students (including student-athletes) may not make recruiting telephone calls to you unless the calls are made as a part of an institution's regular admissions program directed at all prospective students. Enrolled students (including student-athletes) may receive telephone calls at your expense on or after June 15 before your senior year.

Contacts

A college coach may contact you in person off the college campus but only on or after June 15 before your senior year.

Any face-to-face meeting between a coach and you or your parents, during which any of you say more than "hello" is a contact. Furthermore, any face-to-face meeting that is prearranged, or occurs at your high school or at any competition or practice site is a contact, regardless of the conversation. These contacts are not permissible "bumps."

In all sports, coaches may contact you off the college campus three times. However, a coach may visit your high school (with your high-school principal's approval) only once a week during a contact period.

Evaluations

An evaluation is any off-campus activity used to assess your academic qualifications or athletics ability, including a visit to your high school (during which no contact occurs) or watching you practice or compete at any site.

In all sports, coaches may evaluate you an unlimited number of times.

In football and basketball only, there are specified periods when a coach may contact you off the college campus and/or attend your practices and games to evaluate your athletic ability.

[Note: There is a "dead" period (coaches may not contact or evaluate you on or off the college campus) in all sports 48 hours before 7 a.m. on the initial signing date for the National Letter of Intent.]

With the permission of your high school's director of athletics, you may tryout for a college team before enrollment. The tryout must occur in a term other than the term in which the traditional season in the sport occurs or after your high-school eligibility is completed and may include tests to evaluate your strength, speed, agility and sports skills. Except in football, ice hockey, lacrosse, soccer and wrestling, the tryout may include competition.

You may visit a college campus any time at your expense. On such a visit, you may receive three complimentary admissions to a game on that campus, a tour of off-campus practice and competition sites in your sport and other facilities within 30 miles of the campus, and a meal for you and your parents or guardians in the college's on-campus student dining facilities.

Official Visits

During your senior year, you may have one expense-paid (official) visit to a particular campus. You may receive no more than a total of five such visits. This restriction applies even if you are being recruited in more than one sport.

A college may not give you an official visit unless you have provided it with a PSAT, ACT or SAT score from a test taken on a national testing date under national testing conditions.

During your official visit (which may not exceed 48 hours), you may receive round-trip transportation between your home (or high school) and the campus, and you (and your parents) may receive meals and lodging.

You also may receive three complimentary admissions to campus athletics events. In addition, a student host may help you (and your family) become acquainted with campus life. The host may spend $30 per day to cover costs of entertaining you (and your parents, legal guardians or spouse); however, the money may not be used to purchase college souvenirs such as T-shirts or other college mementos.

Printed Materials

A Division II college recruiting you may provide to you printed recruiting materials on or after September 1 at the beginning of your junior year.

In addition, a Division II college may show you a highlight film/videotape, but may not send it to you or leave it with you or your coach.

Finally, a Division II college also may provide you with a questionnaire, camp brochure and educational information published by the NCAA (such as this guide) at any time.

Division III

In addition to general recruiting regulations, you (or your family) may not receive any benefit, inducement or arrangement such as cash, clothing, cars, improper expenses, transportation, gifts or loans to encourage you to attend any NCAA school.

An athletics department staff member, alumni or representative of a college's athletics interests (boosters or representatives) may contact you in person off the college campus after your junior year of high school.

There is no limit on the number of contacts or the period when they may occur. You may not tryout for a Division III college's athletics team. A tryout is any physical activity (e.g., practice session or test) conducted by or arranged on behalf of a college, at which you display your ability.

You can visit a college campus any time at your own expense. On such a visit, you may receive three complimentary admissions to a game on that campus; a tour of off-campus practice and competition sites in your sport and other college facilities within 30 miles of the campus; a meal in the college's on-campus student dining facilities; and housing, if it is available to all visiting prospective students.

Official Visits

During your senior year, you may make one expense-paid (official) visit to a particular campus; however, there is no limit on the number of campuses that you may visit if you initially enroll in a Division III college.

During your official visit (which may not exceed 48 hours), you may receive round-trip transportation between your home (or high school) and the campus, and you (and your parents) may receive meals, lodging and complimentary admissions to campus athletics events. All meals provided to you (and/or your parents) on an official visit must occur in an on-campus dining facility that the college's students normally use. If dining facilities are closed, the college is permitted to take you off-campus for meals. In addition, a student host may help you (and your family) become acquainted with campus life. The host may spend $20 per day to cover all costs of entertaining you (and your parents, legal guardians or spouse); however, the money can't be used to purchase college souvenirs such as T-shirts or other college mementos.

Printed Materials

A Division III college is permitted at anytime to provide you, your high-school, and/or two-year college coach any official academic, admissions, athletics and student-services publications published by the college and other general information available to all students.

NCAA Division I Recruiting Calendars

All contacts and evaluations must adhere to the recruiting calendar established for each particular sport. A coach may only contact you off the college campus and/or attend your practices and games to evaluate your athletic ability during a designated contact or evaluation period. Consult the recruiting calendars to determine when contact and evaluations are permissible for your sport. You may view the current NCAA Recruiting Calendars by using the link provided below

www.ncaa.org/wps/wcm/connect/public/NCAA/Resources/Recruiting+Calendars

Tips on Recruiting

- Select a college for academic reasons first. Sports will not pay your bills when you are 40 years old, but a good college education will.

- Select different types of schools to look at. Mix your choices between small and large, urban and rural, near home and far away. This way, you will have distinct choices from which to choose.

- When making visits to schools, find out as much as you can about their program. Get away from the sports athletic office and get to know as many team members as you can. By doing so, you can find out about such things as practice, academic conflicts, coaches' personalities, faculty, graduation rate and study halls.

- Fill out your "College Information Sheets" while on your visits. Don't rely on your memory as you approach the decision making time.

- Be honest with coaches at all times. If you are not interested at the beginning, tell them. It will save both of you a lot of time. One of the most difficult things you will have to do, if you are fortunate enough to receive multiple scholarship offers, is to say "NO" to all but one of the schools. Don't give in to pressure. Do what you feel is right.

- If a school pressures you to sign anything before the "National Letter of Intent Signing Date", it is illegal and unethical. You may verbally commit to a school before that date, but don't do so under the threat of pressure. "We'll pull our scholarship offer away if you don't commit now" is an unacceptable practice, but it will occur.

- Listen to the opinion of others, but realize that this is the first major decision YOU will have to live with. Don't do it on a whim or a fancy. Instead base it on sound logic and thorough preparation.

- Once you have made your decision, doubt is inevitable. If you are 80% sure, grab the offer and run!

10 Most Important Recruiting Questions in the World

For the Parent:

1. Where is my student-athlete on your "Recruiting List" and do you plan on offering them any financial aid or scholarship. (Then zip it.... The next words should come out of the college coaches' mouth and those words will tell you a lot about that college coach and their interest level in your student-athlete)

2. If you offer my student-athlete a scholarship how long will the offer be good for. (There are 2 answers to this question. #1 – The college coach says "Let your student-athlete take as much time as they need". We want him/her and don't want to put any pressure on them. #2 – The coach says "I'm giving you 10 days"! (that tells you something totally different. Your athlete isn't their top pick and this coach is already putting PRESSURE on your athlete. If they're putting pressure on them even before they commit to this college, what do you think will happen when your athlete gets to that college. That coach will more than likely put pressure on your athlete every day. NOT GOOD ☺).

For the Student-Athlete:

3. Does the college have the major or course studies you want to take in college?

4. How far are you willing to travel to go to college? Across country, 3-hour radius from home? (The smaller the circle the fewer colleges and opportunities you will have.

5. Do you want to go to a smaller college, under 10,000 under grads or larger over 15,000?

6. Are you willing to wait a few years to get on the field or court or do you want to play early? (This is one of the most important decisions you will make. Most athletes that go to a larger D-I or D-II college will sit out at least one or two years before getting their shot as a junior or senior because the talent level of the upper classmen ahead of them on the roster is very high. Going to a smaller D-III college will probably allow you to get playing time much earlier).

7. Are you flexible with the position that you will ultimately play in college? (If you are flexible you will probably play a lot sooner than if you stick to one position. Some coaches needs change or they get a recruit that was an All-American that plays your position).

8. How important is it to you whether or not your parents will be able to see you play?

9. How important is the head coach in making your decision? (Coaches change colleges often. If you are making your decision mainly based on the coach you could be very disappointed. Of course, the coach should be a part of your decision, but don't allow it to be more than 50%).

10. Finally, before you commit to a college, ask yourself this question.... If I go to this college and the first day of practice my freshman year and God forbid you were to have a career ending injury, would you still want to go to that college for 4 or 5 years to get your EDUCATION? (If your answer is YES then you found the right school. If your answer is NO then keep looking)!

COMMITTING

An institution may indicate in writing or by phone to a prospect that an athletics grant-in-aid (athletic scholarship) will be offered by the institution. However, the prospect may not sign a form indicating the prospect's acceptance of such an award before the initial signing date for the National Letter of Intent.

Verbal Acceptance

If an institution makes a scholarship offer prior to the official signing date, the prospect may publicly announce they are verbally committing to that institution. This, however, may not stop other institutions from trying to change their mind. A verbal commitment is not a binding agreement unlike the National Letter of Intent. Although by making a verbal commitment it does not bind the student-athlete to the college, it does in a realistic sense bind the college to the student-athlete. (not legally, just realistically). By making an early verbal commitment to a college the student-athlete has a sort of "insurance policy" in the event he or she is injured prior to entering college. Most colleges have insurance policies covering such injuries to prospects that have verbally committed. They will normally honor a scholarship offer to a student-athlete whose career is ended by an injury just simply because it is the right thing to do.

Written Acceptance

The National Letter of Intent is a document which is managed by the NCAA, but is governed by the Collegiate Commissioners Association. The basic premise of the National Letter of Intent (NLI) program is to provide finality to the recruiting process. Most colleges that offer NCAA Division I and II athletic scholarships use the NLI. No Division III schools, NAIA schools, junior colleges or preparatory schools are members of the NLI Program. However, many NAIA institutions and junior colleges do use a Letter of Intent, implemented either by the national association, their individual conferences, or even individual schools.

During each academic year, there are several signing periods. Depending on the sport there may be either one or two signing periods. If the sport has two periods they are designated as the early and the late signing periods. The early period occurs for one week in November, while the late signing period starts around the second week of April and continues for a month. If the sport only has one signing period it usually starts in early February and continues until August 1st. Although a college may offer a scholarship before February, the recruit may not sign that official letter until the signing period.

Signing the National Letter of Intent, in effect, ends the recruiting process. Member schools agree to not pursue a student-athlete once they sign a NLI with another institution. However, not all college coaches abide by this part of the agreement. After signing the NLI, the prospect is also ensured an athletic scholarship for one academic year. An institutional financial aid tender accompanies the NLI. If the student-athlete does not enroll at that school for a complete academic year, they could be penalized, with the possibility of losing up to two seasons of eligibility.

A student-athlete signs a National Letter of Intent with an institution and not with a specific coach. If the coach who recruited the student-athlete leaves that institution, the NLI is still valid and they are legally bound to the school for one full year. If a high school prospect signs a National Letter of Intent and then reneges on the contract and does not attend the school or does not satisfy the terms of the NLI Program, they lose two years of eligibility at the next NLI institution. But, if the school they leave agrees to enter into a Qualified Release Agreement, the penalty is reduced from two years to one. The original school is not required to provide the student-athlete with the Qualified Release Agreement. However, many coaches will grant a release if a player wishes to leave. If a student-athlete signs it on a day outside of the early or late signing period, the NLI agreement is null and void.

There is a big difference between the National Letter of Intent and other Letters of Intent, such as those used by NAIA schools or junior colleges. If a recruit signs an NLI and later decides to instead enroll at an NAIA institution or junior college, there are no penalties. The reverse is also true – if a student-athlete signs a Letter of Intent at an NAIA school or junior college, they can change their mind and later sign a National Letter of Intent without having to sit out for a year. Only after signing an NLI and then changing from one NCAA Division I or II institution to another would they lose a season or seasons of eligibility.

When a prospect signs a National Letter of Intent, they are guaranteed athletic financial aid for one academic year at that institution and nothing more. By attending the college with which the student-athlete signed for at least one academic year, and not just by completing one playing season at that school, they satisfy the NLI. A student-athlete only signs a National Letter of Intent one time, but they sign the financial tender every year.

QUESTIONS TO ASK WHEN CHOOSING A COLLEGE

UNIVERSITY

- Distance from home?
- Is the university in an urban or rural setting?
- What is the student enrollment?
- What is the size of the campus?
- What are the residence halls like?
- Must students live on campus?
- What are the campus activities?
- Is this university a commuter or residential campus?
- What is the vision/mission statement of the university?
- Is the campus safe? Is it a friendly environment?

ACADEMICS

- Does this university have my major?
- How many years will it take me to get through my major?
- How strong is my major at this university?
- What is the student to professor ratio? What is the average class size?
- What is the graduation rate for the university, students in my major, athletes, the program?
- What percent of graduates are placed out of my major?
- Do student-athletes get priority scheduling?
- Is tutorial help available? Writing center? Are study tables required?
- Are professors willing to work with the schedule of an athlete?
- Does the coach monitor grades / class attendance? How?

THE PROGRAM

- What is the vision/core values of the program?
- What kind of tradition has the program established?
- What level of commitment has been made to the program by the university/ athletic department?
- How strong is the conference?
- What was the win/loss record last season? Over the past 5 seasons?
- Where did the team finish in the conference last year? Over the past 5 years?
- Did any team member receive All-Conference recognition? All-American recognition?

THE COACH / TEAM

- How long has the coaching staff been there?
- When does the head coach's contract end?
- What best describes the head coach's style of coaching?

- What is the player/coach relationship like?
- What kind of "team building" activities does the team do?
- What is the style of play?
- Do freshmen get an opportunity to play? Is "redshirting" an option?
- Do the players get along?
- How are captains selected?
- What are the team's yearly goals? Who decides them?
- Does the team get support from the student body? From the community?
- Does the team have a full time athletic trainer? Does he/she travel with the team?
- Is the team involved in community service activities?

TRAVEL/ COMPETITION SCHEDULE

- How does the team travel? Farthest road trip?
- Where does the team stay on road trips? How many to a room?
- How many classes (on the average) are missed first semester? Second semester?
- What does the non-conference schedule look like?
- Does the team play in any tournament?
- On what days does competition take place?
- Does the team play double-headers? How many?
- Does the university have the opportunity to host the conference tournament? Regional tournament? National tournament?
- Will there be an opportunity to take a "nice trip" during my career here?

FACILITIES

- What is the locker room like?
- Does the team have its own team/film room?
- Does the team practice and play games in the same facility?
- What is the weight room like? How many teams share it?

SCHOLARSHIPS

- What is covered by the scholarship?
- When would a scholarship not be renewed?
- What would happen to the scholarship if a career ending injury occurs?
- What are preferred, invited and uninvited walk-on situations? How many earn a scholarship?

STUDENT-ATHLETE'S SCHEDULE

Are these required of an athlete in the program?
Summers spent on campus taking classes?
Work summer camps?

– "Whether on the court or off, Coach Ramsey, leads by example. Her commitment to excellence is shadowed only by her deep and abiding faith. Retired from a 35 year coaching career, 20 of which she served as head coach for the Ashland University Women's Basketball Team. She led the Ashland Eagles to a Division

2 national title in 2013, which followed on the heels of being 2012 national runner-up. That same year Coach Ramsey was named the 2012 Conference, Regional and NCAA Division 2 National Coach of the Year and inducted into Miami University's prestigious Cradle of Coaches.

It is now Coach's passion to share her life experiences with others to inspire, encourage, and motivate them to pursue their God-given purpose with joy, humility, and gratitude."

Letter of Intent Frequently Asked Questions

Q. When I sign a National Letter of Intent what do I agree to do?

When you sign the National Letter of Intent you agree to attend for one academic year the institution listed on the Letter in exchange for that institution awarding athletics financial aid for one academic year.

Q. By signing a National Letter of Intent am I guaranteed that I will play on a team?

No. Signing a National Letter of Intent does not guarantee you playing time or a spot on the team. Rather, by signing a National Letter of Intent, the institution with which you sign agrees to provide you athletics financial aid for the academic year.

Q. How do I fulfill the National Letter of Intent?

You fulfill the National Letter of Intent in one of two ways: (1) By attending the institution with which you sign for at least one academic year; or, (2) By graduating from a junior college if you signed a National Letter of Intent while in high school or during your first year at the junior college.

Q. If I complete the playing season at the institution with which I sign, have I fulfilled the National Letter of Intent?

No. Completing a playing season alone does not fulfill the National Letter of Intent. You must complete the academic year in residence.

Q. Do I sign a National Letter of Intent every year?

No, while under NCAA rules you must be notified annually regarding whether your athletics aid has been renewed. You only sign an NLI when you first enroll in a four-year institution or if you are a four-two-four transfer student.

Q. Once I sign a National Letter of Intent may I be recruited by other institutions?

Once you sign a National Letter of Intent, all other participating conferences and institutions are obligated to cease recruiting you. Accordingly, you have an obligation to notify any recruiter from a National Letter of Intent institution of the fact you have signed a National Letter of Intent.

Q. Am I required to sign a National Letter of Intent?

No. You are not required to sign a National Letter of Intent but many student-athletes sign a National Letter of Intent because they want to create certainty in the recruiting process. Specifically, by signing a National Letter of Intent, you agree to attend the institution for one year in exchange for the institution's promise, in writing, to provide you athletics financial aid for the entire academic year. Simply, by signing a National Letter of Intent you are given an award including athletics aid for the upcoming academic year provided you are admitted to the institution and you are eligible for athletics aid under NCAA rules. Furthermore, by signing a National Letter of Intent you effectively end the recruiting process. Once you sign a National Letter of Intent, a recruiting ban goes into effect and you may no longer be recruited by any other National Letter of Intent school.

Q. If I sign with an NCAA Division I institution may I still sign with a Division II institution?

The true issue is not whether a school is a Division I or Division II institution but whether an institution is a member of the National Letter of Intent Program. With more than 500 participating institutions, the NLI program is truly national in scope. Briefly, all Division I institutions, with the exception of the Service Academies, half of the Patriot League and schools in the Ivy League, are members of the program, and all fully active Division II institutions participate in the program. No Division III institutions, NAIA schools, preparatory schools, junior colleges, or community colleges participate in the National Letter of Intent program.

Q. If I sign a National Letter of Intent in one sport may I sign a National Letter of Intent in a different sport?

No. You may only sign one valid National Letter of Intent annually. Furthermore, when you sign a National Letter of Intent, the Letter is signed with an institution and not with a coach or with a specific sports team.

Generally, only prospective student-athletes enrolling in a four-year institution for the first time sign a National Letter of Intent. Student-athletes who start their academic career at a four-year institution and then transfer to a junior college may also sign a National Letter of Intent if they plan on entering a second four-year institution.

Q. Is a National Letter of Intent considered valid if I submit it to the institution via facsimile?

Yes. When you sign the National Letter of Intent, you enter into an agreement with the institution. Faxing only represents the means by which you transmit the National Letter. Accordingly, a National Letter of Intent transmitted by facsimile is considered valid. In addition to sending the fax, you should also return the hard copy of the National Letter to the signing institution.

Q. If I do not live with a parent or legal guardian, is it necessary that a parent or legal guardian sign the National Letter of Intent?

If you are under the age of 21, your parent or legal guardian must sign the National Letter of Intent in order for it to be considered valid. If you are 21 years of age or older, it is not necessary for your parent or legal guardian to sign the document.

Q. If my parent or legal guardian lives at a different location than I do, is it permissible to sign a letter sent by facsimile?

While not ideal, it is permissible to obtain signatures on a National Letter of Intent via fax. From a procedural stand point, you should make three copies of the fax and sign the document in triplicate. Once signed, you should retain a copy for your records and return the other two copies to the institution. When the institution receives the copies, they will retain a copy and forward a copy to their conference office for filing.

Q. May a coach be present when I sign the National Letter of Intent off-campus?

No. A coach cannot be present when you sign a National Letter of Intent off-campus. Pursuant to NCAA Bylaw 13.1.6.2, any in-person, off-campus contact made with a prospect for the purpose of signing a National Letter of Intent or attendance at activities related to the signing of the National Letter of Intent is prohibited.

Q. Is it permissible to receive a National Letter of Intent while on campus for an official visit?

Yes. While under the terms of the National Letter of Intent program a coach or institutional representative may not hand-deliver a National Letter of Intent off-campus, there is nothing that precludes you from receiving a National Letter of Intent while on campus for an official visit. Please remember that you may only sign a National Letter of Intent during a permissible signing period. Furthermore, signing a National Letter of Intent is a big commitment. Accordingly, it is strongly suggested that you consult your parent or legal guardian in this decision-making process.

Q. If I am going to walk-on to the team, may I sign a National Letter of Intent?

No. Under the terms of the National Letter of Intent program, an institution is strictly prohibited from allowing you to sign a National Letter of Intent if you are a non-scholarship walk-on. In order for a National Letter of Intent to be considered valid, it must be accompanied by an athletics financial aid award letter, which lists the terms and conditions of the award, including the amount and duration of the financial aid. Simply put, there must be an athletics aid award including athletics aid for a National Letter of Intent to be valid.

Q. May I sign a National Letter of Intent before I am certified as eligible by the NCAA Eligibility Center?

Yes. However your NLI requires your Eligibility Center ID to be valid. You may sign a National Letter of Intent before you receive your final certification determination from the NCAA Eligibility Center, but you need to register with the Eligibility Center before signing. In fact, it is very common for a prospect to sign a National Letter of Intent during the course of his/her senior year. When you sign a National Letter of Intent you agree to submit the necessary information and documents to the NCAA Eligibility Center. If you are classified by the NCAA Eligibility Center as either a Qualifier or Partial Qualifier, the National Letter of Intent is considered valid. If by the institution's opening day of classes for the fall term you are classified as a non-qualifier pursuant to NCAA Bylaw 14.3, your National Letter of Intent is rendered null and void.

Q. When is the permissible time period for signing a National Letter of Intent?

You may sign a National Letter of Intent only during the designated signing period. If you sign a National Letter of Intent outside the appropriate signing period, the National Letter of Intent shall be considered null and void. Presuming you are within the permissible signing period, you and your parent or legal guardian must sign the NLI within 14 days of issuance

Q. Where is my signed National Letter of Intent filed? Who is responsible for filing the document?

You should sign your National Letter of Intent in triplicate. Once you have signed the Letter in triplicate, you should retain one copy of the signed Letter for your records. You should then send the remaining two documents to the institution listed on the Letter. When the institution receives your Letters, it will keep one copy and forward one copy to its conference office. The institution must file your NLI with its conference office within 21 days after the date of final signature. If this filing deadline is not met, the Letter will be invalid. Once the conference office receives your Letter, it will notify the National Letter of Intent office via mail or computer of the fact you have signed a National Letter of Intent.

Q. Is a National Letter of Intent binding if the coach of my sport leaves the institution to take another position?

Yes. The National Letter of Intent you signed with an institution is valid if the coach that recruited you leaves the institution with which you signed. When you sign a National Letter of Intent you sign with an institution and not with a coach or team.

Q. Do I sign a National Letter of Intent if I transfer to another four-year institution?

No. A student-athlete transferring from one four-year institution to another four-year institution may not sign a National Letter of Intent.

Q. What happens if I change my mind and do not want to attend the institution with which I sign and want to attend another National Letter of Intent institution?

If you do not attend the institution with which you signed, or if you do not fulfill the terms of the National Letter of Intent, the basic penalty is that you lose two years of eligibility and must serve two years in residence at your next National Letter of Intent institution.

Q. May the Basic Penalty, which calls for the loss of two years of eligibility and requires that I serve two years in residence at the next National Letter of Intent Institution, be reduced?

Yes. The Basic Penalty under the National Letter of Intent agreement may be reduced by entering into a Qualified Release Agreement with the signing institution. By entering into a Qualified Release Agreement, the institution and the student-athlete mutually agree to release each other from any commitment and liability related to signing a National Letter of Intent. Pursuant to the Qualified Release Agreement, you may not represent a second National Letter of Intent institution in any sport during your first year of residence and you will be charged with the loss of one season of eligibility in all sports

Q. Who executes the Qualified Release Agreement?

The Qualified Release Agreement must be executed by the Director of Athletics (or a designee), your parent or legal guardian and yourself. Your coach does not sign the Qualified Release Agreement. Furthermore, your coach does not have the authority to release you from your National Letter of Intent obligations.

Q. Is the Qualified Release Agreement the same as the One-Time Transfer Exception as set forth in NCAA Bylaw 14.5.5.2.10?

No. The Qualified Release Agreement and the NCAA One-Time Transfer Exception are two different policies. A student-athlete who has not previously transferred from a four-year institution and does not participate in the sports of Division I basketball, Division I-A football or Division I men's ice hockey, may transfer and not have to serve a year in residence under NCAA rules. To use the One-Time Transfer Exception, the student-athlete must have been in good academic standing and fulfilled progress toward degree requirements at the previous institution. Furthermore, the student-athlete must have been eligible at the previous institution and the previous institution must have no objection to the student being granted an exception to the NCAA residence requirement. The fact that a student is eligible for the NCAA One-Time Transfer Exception does not mean a student-athlete has received a Qualified Release Agreement pursuant to the National Letter of Intent program, nor does the One-Time Transfer Exception eliminate the penalty provisions of the National Letter of Intent.

Q. Is an institution required to grant a Qualified Release Agreement if requested?

No. Just as the National Letter of Intent is a voluntary agreement, the Qualified Release Agreement is voluntary in nature. An institution is not required to provide you with a Qualified Release Agreement. If an institution denies your request for a Qualified Release Agreement, you may petition the National Letter of Intent Steering Committee for such an agreement. In order to petition the NLI Steering Committee, you must document in writing that you requested a Qualified Release Agreement from the Director of Athletics of the signing institution and that your request was denied. Once proper documentation has been submitted, the NLI Steering Committee will consider your request.

Q. If I do not satisfy my National Letter of Intent agreement, may I practice or receive athletics aid at another National Letter of Intent institution?

Yes. Signing a National Letter of Intent does not impact your ability to practice or receive athletics aid at another National Letter of Intent institution. The Basic Penalty under the National Letter of Intent program is the loss of two years of eligibility in all sports and the requirement of two years in residence at the next National Letter of Intent institution.

Q. If I fail to honor my NLI commitment and do not attend the institution with which I signed, may another NLI member institution recruit me?

Yes, but only if you have received a Qualified Release Agreement from the institution with which you signed, or the institution that desires to recruit you is granted permission to do so by the institution with which you signed. (If permission to contact is granted, it is not limited to certain institutions, but to all institutions seeking to recruit the student-athlete.)

Q. If my request for a Qualified Release Agreement is denied, is the institution obligated to provide me an opportunity for a hearing as to why the request was denied?

No.

Q. May a mid-year enrollee sign a National Letter of Intent?

Under the terms of the National Letter of Intent program, a written award of athletics aid for the entire academic year must accompany a National Letter of Intent. Accordingly, the National Letter of Intent program does not allow for prospective student-athletes enrolling at midyear to sign a National Letter of Intent. The National Letter of Intent program has created an exception to this general rule for midyear junior college transfer students in the sport of football. A midyear junior college transfer student in the sport of football may sign a National Letter of Intent during the designated signing period.

Q. If I sign a letter of intent with a junior college or an NAIA school may I sign a National Letter of Intent?

Yes. You may sign a National Letter of Intent if you have already signed a letter of intent with a junior college or an NAIA school. By entering the National Letter of Intent program, participating institutions agree to honor one another's commitments. Make certain you understand the difference between a NAIA or junior college letter and the National Letter of Intent before you sign more than one letter.

Q. If I sign a National Letter of Intent, may I attend an NAIA school or a school that does not participate in the NLI program without incurring any National Letter of Intent penalties?

If you sign a National Letter of Intent, you may attend any institution that does not belong to the National Letter of Intent program without incurring any National Letter of Intent penalties while at the non-participating school. Please note, though, if you ever transfer to an institution participating in the National Letter of Intent program, the National Letter of Intent penalties would be applied at your next National Letter of Intent institution.

Q. If I call the NCAA may I get more information about the National Letter of Intent?

No. The National Letter of Intent program is not administered by the NCAA. Rather, the National Letter of Intent program is administered by the Collegiate Commissioners Association (CCA). The CCA was formed in 1939 to promote uniformity in football officiating and mechanics and to standardize interpretations of playing rules throughout the nation. Over the years the CCA has grown, but its mission has remained consistent over time, promoting uniformity and standard treatment of issues. By promoting uniform treatment of prospective student-athletes, the National Letter of Intent program reduces and limits recruiting pressure on student-athletes and promotes and preserves the amateur nature of collegiate athletics. Conferences, on behalf of their member institutions, join the National Letter of Intent program and are knowledgeable about National Letter of Intent rules and regulations. The Southeastern Conference handles the daily administrative duties of the National Letter of Intent program on behalf of the CCA.

Q. Where may I find more information about the National Letter of Intent?

While certainly this web site is an excellent place to find information regarding the National Letter of Intent, the best way to learn about the document is to read the actual letter. All the terms of the National Letter of Intent have been published on the document so you can have time to read and understand the terms of the agreement. Signing a National Letter of Intent is a very important step and you owe it to yourself to read the document and to review it with your parent or legal guardian. When you sign a National Letter of Intent you are agreeing to attend the institution with which you sign for one academic year. Accordingly, you should be certain about your choice of institution before you sign a National Letter of Intent.

NCAA National Letter of Intent Signing Dates

Each sport has a designated signing period, while some sports have two periods. Football, Field Hockey Soccer, Track & Field, Cross Country, and Men's Water Polo only have one signing period. All other sports have an early period and a regular period. The early period is traditionally in November and only last about a week. The regular signing period last at least a month, but often more. A complete listing of the signing periods can be found by using the following link.

www.thestudentathleteandcollegerecruiting.com/more_resources

Walking-On as an Option

What is a "Walk-on"?

A "WALK-ON" is a student-athlete that goes to college and participates in a sport without any athletic financial aid. In other words, NO SCHOLARSHIP! Many athletic programs around the country use walk-ons as an integral part of their team. For instance, in Division I football with the number of scholarships limited to 85, most programs could not function without walk-ons. In fact many colleges encourage them. After all, it doesn't cost the college any scholarship money and yet they benefit from having these fine athletes to help round out their team. I'm going to describe three different scenarios in which an athlete considers, or maybe even benefits from being a walk-on.

1. Maybe you have always wanted to play football for the Fighting Irish of Notre Dame. But in high school they never recruited you. Even though you were recruited by some other Division I football programs, and perhaps even offered scholarships by some, your heart always came back to Notre Dame. You contacted their recruiting coordinator and although they were interested in you, they had already offered a scholarship to another athlete at your same position. Still, you wanted to play for Notre Dame. You asked the coaches if they would allow you to walk-on and be a part of the practice squad. It was more important to play where your heart was even if it meant paying for your education. They invited you and said that if you proved you could help their team, there may be scholarship money available for you next year. BUT NO PROMISES! This scenario happens quite often and there is nothing wrong with it. Just because the school of your dreams doesn't need you right out of high school, that doesn't mean they won't need you a year or two down the road. **Sometimes it's more important to follow your HEART!**

2. All through high school you thought you were a Division I athlete. But, you weren't honest and realistic in evaluating your talent. You set your sights TOO

HIGH. You were a Division II athlete at best. So you shunned the Division II and III colleges that were interested in hopes that the Division I offers were coming. The offers never came and you were left with nothing. Even the few Division II schools that were offering scholarships earlier, couldn't wait any longer and they gave your scholarship money to someone else. This also happens to many high school athletes. The only thing left to do is "walk-on" at a school and hope for the best.

3. You were always too small, too slow and never strong enough to compete with the big boys. Finally, your senior year, you started on the varsity squad. But there was no way you could ever expect to receive athletic scholarship money from any school. You really enjoyed participating in athletics and didn't want it to end at high school. You decided to find a Division III college that would accept you onto their team as a "walk-on". After all, you were a hard worker, a very good student, and were very coachable. Remember that a college never has enough scholarship players to fill all their needs. An example would be the practice or dummy squad. These squads pretend to be next weeks' opposing team so the first team offense and defense can better prepare for the game. And, it's a lot safer to have walk-ons getting beat around, than to have your scholarship players being injured. I know that sounds cruel but - THAT'S HOW IT IS!

Being a walk-on can be very rewarding and satisfying. But it can also be very stressful. I knew of a young lady from Pennsylvania who was a fantastic soccer player in high school. She had one scholarship offer from a Division II school and lots of interest from Division III schools. Despite all these signs, she believed that she could compete at the Division I level. So, she passed up the D-II and D-III offers and decided to walk-on to a Division I school in hopes of getting a scholarship and of course playing time down the road. In her four years at the Division I school, she never once set foot on the soccer field competitively except for practices. WHAT A MISTAKE!

I also knew a young man from Ohio who shunned D-II and D-III schools to pursue his dream of playing Division I football. Not only did he receive a FULL ATHLETIC SCHOLARSHIP his sophomore year, but by the time he was a senior he was elected Captain of the team. WHAT A SUCCESS STORY!

Just so there is no misunderstanding, you need to know the following:

- A walk-on athlete must participate in all the practices, drills and out-of-season workouts that the scholarship players do. Most often the "walk-on" athletes hardly ever step onto the playing field.

- When you consider the time and energy needed to practice and/or compete, along with the academic load, and the fact that YOU are paying for your college education, it can be extremely difficult to go this route.

Where do you fit into these scenarios? Is it a gamble to pass up scholarships to other schools and go the walk-on route at another? Absolutely! Can it be the perfect answer for some student-athletes? You bet! It's up to you to choose which road to follow. As you can see, it takes a very special person to be a WALK-ON!

But hey, did you ever hear of a guy named RUDY?

After you Commit

As you go through the recruiting process, you will develop a relationship with the college coach that will ultimately become a major factor in choosing or not choosing their university. The coach seems to like you a lot and they talk about how you are going to help their program win next year as a freshman. They emphasize the **"family atmosphere"** that exists in their athletic program and how the coaching staff takes pride in considering each athlete as "one of their own". They tell your parents to call anytime if there are any problems or concerns. And they encourage your parents to visit their campus often so they may enjoy your college career.

THIS IS ALL PART OF THE RECRUITING PROCESS!

The facts are that very few freshmen ever walk on to a college campus and play immediately regardless of how good they think they are, or how good the college coach says they are. There is so much to learn and prepare for both physically and mentally, not to mention the rigorous academic load that you will have in college. There will **DEFINITELY** be a period of adjustment. It will also be very difficult to compete with the other athletes on the team that have been there for two, three, or even four years. But don't worry about not playing your freshman year. I believe that **ALL** athletes should be redshirted their freshman year. (Redshirt means that you can practice with the team but not step onto the athletic field for competition, leaving you with four years of eligibility.) It will give you time to adjust to college life and being away from home for probably the first time in your life. And, don't forget that could be one more year of free education you will receive. And although your parents were encouraged to visit you whenever possible when you get to college the coach will want you to have as few distractions as possible. **THAT INCLUDES YOUR PARENTS!** Parents need to be prepared for this change in attitude or it will also be a difficult transition for them. Remember, it's the college coaches' job to attract you to their university. When the National Letter of Intent signing date arrives and you legally commit yourself in writing to attend their university, to some degree, more or less, your relationship with the college coach **WILL CHANGE!** And so will the relationship between your parents and the coach.

THE HONEYMOON IS OVER!

TRANSFERRING

The purpose of this section is to familiarize you with the regulations involved with transferring from one educational institution to another. Some students will decide for personal, academic or financial reasons, to begin their post-high school education at a two-year college. At some point, maybe a year or two after enrollment at such a school, it may be time to transfer to a four-year Division I or II college. In order to do this, it is very important that you are familiar with the rules governing such a transfer. You also need to be cautious in that sometimes conference eligibility rules may be more stringent than NCAA rules. The following is to be used as a guide when you are considering such a move. However, it is critical that you contact others while in this process, including your college director of athletics and the college's conference office to make certain that you are on the right track. Any mistakes that you make regarding this transfer could affect your eligibility to practice, compete, or receive athletic financial aid at your new school.

If you need assistance in determining your transfer status you can check with the NCAA Eligibility Center. Representatives there can help you evaluate your academic record to determine if you are a qualifier. They can be reached at 877.262.1492 or at www.eligibilitycenter.org.

Two Year College Transfer

If you are now in a two-year school, never previously attended a four-year school, and want to transfer to a four-year school, we sometimes refer to you as a **2-4** transfer. Here are the rules that generally apply to you.

Division I Schools

First, you must determine whether you were a qualifier or non-qualifier at the end of high school. If you need help determining this, contact the NCAA Eligibility Center, your high school guidance counselor or coach.

If you were a **qualifier**, you must meet the following in order to compete at the Division I level:

- Complete at least one term as a full-time student? Summer school doesn't count.

- Earn an average of 12-semester or 12-quarter credit hours for each term you started fulltime? These credit hours must be transferable toward your degree at the four-year school.

- Have a cumulative GPA of 2.000.

If you answered **YES** to all three requirements then you may practice, receive financial aid, and play immediately at the D-I school. However, if you answered

NO to any of the requirements then you may be able to practice and receive financial aid as long as you are enrolled as a full-time student and meet conference and college regulations. You may not play until you complete one full academic year of residence.

If you were a **non-qualifier,** at the two-year school did you:

- Complete at least three semesters or four quarters as a full time student? Summer school does not count.
- Earn an Associate of Arts degree? You must earn 25 percent of the credit hours at the two-year school that awards your degree.
- Earn 48-semester or 72-quarter credit hours? These credit hours must be transferable toward your degree at the four year school.
- Have a cumulative GPA of 2.000?

If you answered **YES** to all four requirements then you may practice, receive financial aid, and play immediately at the D-I school. However, if you answered **NO** to any of the requirements you may not **practice, compete, or receive financial aid** until you complete one full year of residence at the Division I school.

Division II Schools

If you are a 2-4 transfer and want to attend a D-II school, you must first determine whether you were a qualifier, partial qualifier, or non-qualifier at the end of high school. If you need help determining this, contact your high school guidance counselor.

If you were a **qualifier**, at the two-year school did you:

- Spend one full-time semester or quarter at the two-year school?
- Have a cumulative GPA of 2.000?
- Complete an average of 12-semester or 12-quarter credit hours for each full-time term? These credits must be transferable toward your degree at the four-year school.

If you answered **YES** to all three requirements then you may practice, receive financial aid, and play immediately at the D-II school. If you answered **NO** to any of the requirements then you may be able to practice and receive financial aid as long as you are enrolled as a full-time student and meet conference and college regulations. You may not play until you complete one full academic year of residence.

If you were a **partial qualifier or a non-qualifier**, at the two-year school did you:

- Complete at least two full semesters as a full-time student?
- Earn an Associate of Arts degree? You must earn 25 percent of the credit hours at the two-year school that awards your degree.

  OR

- Complete an average of 12-semester or 12-quarter credit hours for each full-time term? These credit hours must be transferable toward your degree at the four-year school.
- Have a cumulative GPA of 2.000?

If you answered **YES** to both requirements then you may practice, receive financial aid, and play at the D-II school. However, if you answered **NO** to at least one requirement then you may not **practice, compete, or receive financial aid** until you complete one full year of residence at the Division II school.

Division III Schools

If you are a 2-4 transfer and want to attend a D-III school, at the two year school did you:

- Practice and play in intercollegiate sports?

If you answered **NO** then you may practice, receive financial aid, and play immediately at the D-III school. However, if you answered **YES** then in order practice, play and receive financial aid, you must have been considered academically and athletically eligible if you had stayed at your two-year school.

Four Year College Transfer

If you are now in a four-year school and want to transfer to another four-year school, we sometimes refer to you as a 4-4 transfer. This rule applies to you:

If you transfer from a four-year school to another four-year school, generally you are not eligible to play at another four-year school until you sit out a year.

However, if you have never transferred before from a four-year school, you might be able to use the one-time transfer exception to play right away at a Division I or II school. To use this exception, you must:

1. Be playing a sport other than Division I Basketball, Division I Men's Ice Hockey, Division I Baseball, or Division I Football.
2. Be in good academic standing and making progress toward your degree.
3. Have been considered eligible if you had stayed in your first school; and
4. Have a written release agreement from your first school saying that it does not object to your receiving an exception to the transfer residence requirement.

Important Points to Consider When Transferring

- Transferable credit hours grade point average is computed by using **all** courses that are transferable to an NCAA school. This includes courses that may not be actually transferable due to the grade earned in them. This is required to be a minimum of 2.000. For example, if you fail a history course that is transferable to an NCAA school, this grade must be included in your GPA calculation, even though the college does not accept the course for credit towards your degree.

- When transferring to a Division I school, you have five calendar years to complete all of your eligible seasons for competition. This calendar clock starts with your first day of full-time enrollment at any institution. Keep in mind, if you opt to stay out of college for two years you will lose those two years of playing eligibility.

- Every student is allowed a maximum of four seasons to compete in their sport. All of your seasons must be used within five calendar years for Division I and ten semesters / fifteen quarters for Division II. **Any** competition (one play in football, etc.) is counted as a full season of competition regardless of the amount of time spent on the playing field. There are some exceptions to this which include a medical hardship waiver, season-of-competition waiver or the two-year college scrimmage exception.

- When transferring to a Division II or III school, you have a maximum of four seasons of competition (or ten semesters / fifteen quarters). The calendar clock does not apply if you stay out of college for a period of time; thus this may be the best option if you need to be out of college for a period of time due to personal, academic or financial reasons.

In conclusion, as mentioned at the beginning of this section on transferring, it is critical to familiarize yourself with the rules and regulations of the NCAA whether you are transferring to a Division I, II or III college. Be sure to use the resources available to you including but not limited to, coaches, athletic directors, and guidance counselors and of course the NCAA Eligibility Center to guide you through this complicated process. It is of utmost importance that you adhere to all of the guidelines set by the NCAA to ensure your ability to practice, compete and receive financial assistance from your new school. Don't forget that the best way to ensure a successful transfer is rigorous preparation on your part.

All Transferring Athletes must obtain their Amateur Certification. If you never registered with the NCAA Eligibility Center, you must do so in order to obtain this certification. There is no reduction in the fee even if you only need the amateur certification.

GLOSSARY

Understanding Key Words & Terms

AAU (Amateur Athletic Union) - The AAU was established in 1888. It is the largest non-profit volunteer organization in the United States and is dedicated to the promotion and development of amateur athletics.

ACT (American College Test) – The ACT is a multiple-choice standardized test that measures your knowledge of some of the subjects taught in high school. The test usually takes about 3 ½ hours.

All-American – A term used to describe the top athlete(s) in a particular sport. There are two types of All-Americans. They are academic and athletic.

Blue Chip Athlete – A student-athlete who is considered one of the top prospects in any given sport and is also highly recruited.

Bump – This is an unscheduled and ILLEGAL contact between a college coach and a prospective student-athlete. This contact may happen outside of the authorized "contact period" mandated by the NCAA. A bump is supposed to be reported to the NCAA although it is considered a minor infraction.

Contact - Any face-to-face meeting between an institution's staff or athletics representative and a prospect (or the prospect's parents or legal guardians) during which any dialogue occurs in excess of a greeting. Also, any face-to-face meeting that is prearranged, or that occurs at a prospect's school or at any competition or practice site, involving the prospect or the prospect's team, is considered a contact, regardless of the conversation that occurs.

Contact period - The period when authorized coaching staff members are permitted to contact and evaluate prospects in person and off your campus.

Dead period - The period when it is not permissible for anyone associated with an institution to contact and evaluate prospects on or off their campus.

Early Signing Period – This is a one-week period in the beginning of November during which student-athletes can sign a National Letter of Intent. Signing this letter commits them to that particular school.

Evaluation - In Division I-A, any off-campus activity designed to assess the academic qualifications or athletic ability of a prospect, including any visit to a prospect's educational institution (during which no contact occurs) or the observation of a prospect participating in any practice or competition at any site.

Evaluation day - In Division I basketball, an evaluation day is defined as one coach engaged in the evaluation of any prospect on 1 day (12:01 a.m. to midnight); 2 coaches making evaluations on the same day use 2 evaluation days. The combined total of such days for all staff members cannot exceed 40.

Evaluation period - The period when authorized coaching staff members are permitted to assess the academic qualifications and athletic ability of prospects off their campus. In-person, off campus recruiting contacts are not permitted during an evaluation period.

Greyshirt - applies to a student athlete who postpones their full time enrollment into an institution (takes below 12 credit hours) for the first year or semester. This provides the greyshirted athlete with 4 years of eligibility remaining.

Full Scholarship – When an institution pays a student-athlete's tuition, room and board, and course-related books and supplies.

Junior College – This refers to a two-year institution that offers three different levels of completion: Associate's Degree (one that enables you to continue in a four-year institution and one that does not) and a vocational certification. Most of these schools are members of the NJCAA (National Junior College Athletic Association).

NAIA – The National Association of Intercollegiate Athletics administers programs and championships similar to the NCAA but for smaller schools.

NCAA – This is the governing body of college athletics. It is consisted of approximately 900 schools that are classified into three divisions.

NCAA Eligibility Center – This center was established by the NCAA in order to verify that a student-athlete has met all the academic and amateurism requirements set by the NCAA before they can compete as a freshman.

NJCAA – The National Junior College Athletic Association is the governing body for junior college athletics.

National Letter of Intent - An official document administered by the Collegiate Commissioning Association, and used by subscribing institutions to establish a prospect's commitment to attend a particular institution.

Official (paid) Visit - A prospect's trip to a campus, paid in whole or in part by that institution.

Prospect (prospective student-athlete) - A student in the ninth grade or above, including students in prep schools and junior colleges and individuals who have officially withdrawn from four-year schools. Any student not yet in the ninth grade becomes a prospect if an institution provides him or her with any financial aid or other benefits that are not generally provided to prospective students.

Proposition 16 – This law was established on August 1, 1995. It sets an eligibility index for student-athletes based on GPA and standardized test-scores.

Proposition 48 – This law states that a student-athlete must meet certain requirements if he/she wants to practice and/or play during their freshman year at a Division I or II school.

Qualifier – This term refers to a student-athlete who has met all the NCAA academic and athletic requirements to be eligible for a scholarship.

Quiet period - The period when authorized institutional staff members are permitted to make in-person contacts with prospects only on their campus. In-person, off-campus contacts and evaluations are not permitted during a quiet period.

Recruiting - Any solicitation of a prospect (or a member of a prospect's family) by an institution's staff or a representative of an athletics interests to encourage the prospect to enroll at that institution and participate in their athletics program.

Redshirt – This term describes a student-athlete who sits out a year of competition. You may still practice and socialize with the team. This can occur due to injury or lack of need for you at the time.

SAT – This is a standardized test that is used as an academic cut-off by the NCAA. There are national testing dates offered throughout the year. The SAT is divided into two basic sections – verbal and math.

Signing Dates – The approved periods of time when a student-athlete is allowed to sign a National Letter of Intent to attend a specific school. These dates are usually the same for all sports except for football and basketball.

Title 9 – This "Education Law" mandates institutions that receive Federal funding, among other things, are not allowed to discriminate on the basis of sex. This law has led to increased funding and opportunities for women's athletics.

Unofficial (nonpaid) Visit - A trip to a campus paid for by a prospect. If an institution or its athletics interests pay for any of your travel expenses or entertainment, the visit becomes official.

Verbal Commitment – When a student-athlete privately or publicly announces they are going to attend a college or university, it is **NOT** a binding commitment on the part of the student-athlete. That only occurs after the signing of the National Letter of Intent. It does however commit, to some degree more or less, the school to the student-athlete.

APPENDIX A

Colleges with Athletics

STATE	D-I	D-II	D-III	NAIA	Oth.	JC
Alabama	9	8	2	4	2	22
Alaska	0	2	0	0	o	0
Arizona	3	1	0	2	1	15
Arkansas	5	6	2	5	1	6
California	24	20	11	18	1	102
Colorado	5	10	1	1	0	6
Connecticut	7	4	9	0	0	4
Delaware	2	2	1	0	0	3
District of Columbia	4	1	3	0	0	0
Florida	13	13	0	10	7	25
Georgia	7	17	8	13	3	16
Hawaii	1	4	0	0	0	0
Idaho	3	1	0	2	0	2
Illinois	13	4	23	11	4	47
Indiana	10	4	10	18	2	2
Iowa	4	1	11	15	2	16
Kentucky	6	4	4	12	1	2
Louisiana	12	0	2	6	0	5
Maine	1	0	11	0	0	6
Maryland	9	2	10	1	1	18
Massachusetts	6	6	45	1	0	11
Michigan	7	9	8	11	2	21
Minnesota	1	9	20	0	3	17
Mississippi	6	1	3	4	0	15
Missouri	5	14	5	14	8	19
Montana	2	1	0	6	1	5
Nebraska	2	4	1	9	4	7
Nevada	2	0	0	0	0	2
New Hampshire	2	3	6	0	2	0

New Jersey	8	4	15	0	0	17
New Mexico	2	3	0	2	1	4
New York	22	16	68	1	3	44
North Carolina	18	22	7	2	4	20
North Dakota	0	2	3	4	1	7
Ohio	13	12	22	7	13	9
Oklahoma	4	12	0	9	2	11
Oregon	4	2	5	7	2	11
Pennsylvania	14	23	59	2	18	17
Rhode Island	4	0	5	0	0	1
South Carolina	12	13	0	5	0	9
South Dakota	2	5	1	4	0	0
Tennessee	12	10	3	8	3	10
Texas	21	15	16	13	1	50
Utah	6	1	0	1	0	3
Vermont	1	1	7	0	0	0
Virginia	15	3	20	1	2	2
Washington	5	4	4	4	1	25
West Virginia	2	14	1	1	1	3
Wisconsin	4	1	25	2	15	1
Wyoming	1	0	0	0	0	7

Note: A D-II or D-III college may have a sport or sports which compete at a higher classification.

College Listings

ALABAMA

NCAA D-I (9)
Alabama A&M University
Alabama State University
Auburn University
Jacksonville State University
Samford University
Troy University
University of Alabama at Birmingham
University of Alabama, Tuscaloosa
University of South Alabama

NCAA D-II (8)
Miles College
Spring Hill College
Stillman College
Tuskegee University
University of Alabama, Huntsville
University of Montevallo
University of North Alabama
University of West Alabama

NCAA D-III (2)
Birmingham-Southern College
Huntingdon College

NAIA (4)
Auburn University, Montgomery
Faulkner University
Talladega College
University of Mobile

Other 4-Year (2)
Concordia College-Selma
Judson College

ALASKA

NCAA D-II (2)
University of Alaska Anchorage
University of Alaska Fairbanks

ARIZONA

NCAA D-I (3)
Arizona State University
Northern Arizona University
University of Arizona

NCAA D-II (1)
Grand Canyon University

NAIA (3)
Embry-Riddle Aeronautical University
Benedictine University at Mesa
Arizona Christian University

Other 4-Year (1)
Southwestern College

ARKANSAS

NCAA D-I (5)
Arkansas State University
University of Arkansas, Fayetteville
University of Arkansas, Little Rock
University of Arkansas, Pine Bluff
University of Central Arkansas

NCAA D-II (6)
Arkansas Tech University
Harding University
Henderson State University
Ouachita Baptist University
Southern Arkansas University
University of Arkansas, Monticello

NCAA D-III (2)
Hendrix College
University of the Ozarks (Arkansas)

NAIA (5)
Central Baptist College
John Brown University
Lyon College
Philander Smith College
Williams Baptist College

Other 4-Year (1)
Arkansas Baptist College

NCAA D-I (24)
California Polytechnic State University
California State Univ., Bakersfield
California State Univ., Fresno
California State Univ., Fullerton
California State Univ., Northridge
California State Univ., Sacramento
Long Beach State University
Loyola Marymount University
Pepperdine University

San Diego State University
San Jose State University
Santa Clara University
St. Mary's College of California
Stanford University
University of California, Berkeley
University of California, Davis
University of California, Irvine
University of California, Los Angeles
University of California, Riverside
University of California, Santa Barbara
University of San Diego
University of San Francisco
University of Southern California
University of the Pacific

NCAA D-II (20)
Academy of Art University
Azusa Pacific University
California Baptist University
California State Polytechnic - Pomona
California State Univ., Chico
California State Univ., Dominguez Hills
California State Univ., East Bay
California State Univ., Los Angeles
California State Univ., Monterey Bay
California State Univ., San Bernardino
California State Univ., Stanislaus
Dominican University
Fresno Pacific University
Holy Names University
Humboldt State University
Notre Dame De Namur University
Point Loma Nazarene University
San Francisco State University
Sonoma State University
University of California, San Diego

NCAA D-III (11)
California Institute of Technology
California Lutheran University
Chapman University
Claremont McKenna Harvey Mudd - Scripps
Mills College
Occidental College
Pomona - Pitzer Colleges
University of California - Santa Cruz
University of La Verne
University of Redlands
Whittier College

NAIA (17)
Biola University
Concordia University
Hope International University
La Sierra University
Marymount California University
Menlo College
Pacific Union College
Providence Christian College
San Diego Christian College
Simpson University
Soka University of America
The Master's College
University of California, Merced
University of Antelope Valley
Vanguard University
Westmont College
William Jessup University

Other 4-Year (1)
Golden State Baptist College

COLORADO

NCAA D-I (5)
Colorado State University
U.S. Air Force Academy
University of Colorado, Boulder
University of Denver
University of Northern Colorado

NCAA D-II (10)
Adams State College
Colorado Christian University
Colorado School of Mines
Colorado State University-Pueblo
Fort Lewis College
Colorado Mesa University
Metropolitan State College of Denver
Regis University
Univ. of Colorado, Colorado Springs
Western State College of Colorado

NCAA D-III (1)
Colorado College

NAIA (1)
Johnson & Wales University

CONNECTICUT

NCAA D-I (7)
Central Connecticut State University
Fairfield University

Quinnipiac University
Sacred Heart University
University of Connecticut
University of Hartford
Yale University

NCAA D-II (4)
Post University
Southern Connecticut State University
University of Bridgeport
University of New Haven

NCAA D-III (9)
Albertus Magnus College
Connecticut College
Eastern Connecticut State University
Mitchell College
St. Joseph College
Trinity College
U.S. Coast Guard Academy
Wesleyan University
Western Connecticut State University

DELAWARE

NCAA D-I (2)
Delaware State University
University of Delaware

NCAA D-II (2)
Goldey-Beacom College
Wilmington College

NCAA D-III (1)
Wesley College

DISTRICT OF COLUMBIA

NCAA D-I (4)
American University
George Washington University
Georgetown University
Howard University

NCAA D-II (1)
University of the District of Columbia

NCAA D-III (3)
Catholic University
Gallaudet University
Trinity College (District of Columbia)

FLORIDA

NCAA D-I (13)
Bethune-Cookman College

Florida A&M University
Florida Atlantic University
Florida Gulf Coast University
Florida International University
Florida State University
Jacksonville University
Stetson University
University of Central Florida
University of Florida
University of Miami
University of North Florida
University of South Florida

NCAA D-II (13)
Barry University
Eckerd College
Embry-Riddle Aeronautical University
Flagler College
Florida Institute of Technology
Florida Southern College
Lynn University
Nova Southeastern University
Palm Beach Atlantic University
Rollins College
Saint Leo University
University of Tampa
University of West Florida

NAIA (9)
Ave Maria University
Edward Waters College
Florida Memorial College
Johnson & Wales University
Keiser University
Saint Thomas University
Southeastern University
Warner University
Webber International University

Other 4-Year (7)
Clearwater Christian College
Florida Christian College
Florida College
Pensacola Christian College
Southeastern University
Trinity Baptist College
Trinity College of Florida

GEORGIA

NCAA D-I (7)
Georgia Institute of Technology

Georgia Southern University
Georgia State University
Kennesaw State University
Mercer University
Savannah State University
University of Georgia

NCAA D-II (17)
Albany State University (Georgia)
Armstrong Atlantic State University
Clark Atlanta University
Clayton College & State University
Columbus State University
Emmanuel College
Fort Valley State University
Georgia Regents University, Augusta
Georgia Southwestern State University
Georgia College & State University
Morehouse College
University of North Georgia
Paine College
Shorter University
University of West Georgia
Valdosta State University
Young Harris College

NCAA D-III (8)
Agnes Scott College
Berry College
Covenant College
Emory University
La Grange College
Oglethorpe University
Piedmont College
Wesleyan College

NAIA (13)
Brenau University
Brewton-Parker College
College of Coastal Georgia
Dalton State College
Georgia Gwinnett College
Life University
Middle Georgia State University
Point University
Reinhardt University
Savannah College of Art & Design, Atlanta
Savannah College of Art & Design, Savannah
Thomas University
Truett - McConnell College

Other 4-Year (3)
Atlanta Christian College
Carver Bible College
Toccoa Falls College

HAWAII

NCAA D-I (1)
University of Hawaii, Manoa

NCAA D-II (4)
Brigham Young University, Hawaii
Chaminade University
Hawaii Pacific University
University of Hawaii, Hilo

IDAHO

NCAA D-I (3)
Boise State University
Idaho State University
University of Idaho

NCAA D-II (1)
Northwest Nazarene University

NAIA (2)
Lewis-Clark State College
The College of Idaho

ILLINOIS

NCAA D-I (13)
Bradley University
Chicago State University
DePaul University
Eastern Illinois University
Illinois State University
Loyola University
Northern Illinois University
Northwestern University
Southern Illinois Univ. at Carbondale
Southern Illinois Univ., Edwardsville
University of Illinois at Chicago
University of Illinois, Champaign
Western Illinois University

NCAA D-II (4)
Lewis University
McKendree University
Quincy University
University of Illinois at Springfield

NCAA D-III (23)
Augustana College
Aurora University

Benedictine University
Blackburn College
Concordia University
Dominican University
Elmhurst College
Eureka College
Greenville College
Illinois College
Illinois Institute of Technology
Illinois Wesleyan University
Knox College
Lake Forest College
Mac Murray College
Millikin University
Monmouth College
North Central College
North Park University
Principia College
Rockford College
University of Chicago
Wheaton College

NAIA (11)
Governor's State University
Judson University
Lincoln Christian University
Lindenwood University
Olivet Nazarene University
Robert Morris University
Roosevelt University
Saint Xavier University
Trinity Christian College
Trinity International University
University of Saint Francis

Other 4-Year (4)
East-West University
Moody Bible Institute
Robert Morris College - Lake County
Robert Morris College - Springfield

INDIANA

NCAA D-I (10)
Ball State University
Butler University
Indiana State University
Indiana University, Bloomington
IU-PU, Indianapolis
IU-PU, Fort Wayne
Purdue University
University of Evansville

University of Notre Dame
Valparaiso University

NCAA D-II (4)
Oakland City University
Saint Joseph's College
University of Indianapolis
University of Southern Indiana

NCAA D-III (10)
Anderson University
DePauw University
Earlham College
Franklin College
Hanover College
Manchester College
Rose-Hulman Institute of Technology
Saint Mary's College
Trine University
Wabash College

NAIA (18)
Bethel College
Calumet College of St. Joseph
Goshen College
Grace College
Holy Cross College
Huntington College
Indiana Institute of Technology
Indiana University East
Indiana University Kokomo
Indiana University Northwest
Indiana University Southeast
Indiana University-South Bend
Indiana Wesleyan University
Marian University
Purdue University Calumet
Purdue University - North Central
Taylor University
University of Saint Francis

Other 4-Year (2)
Saint Mary-of-the-Woods College
Taylor University - Ft. Wayne

IOWA

NCAA D-I (4)
Drake University
Iowa State University
University of Iowa
University of Northern Iowa

NCAA D-II (1)
Upper Iowa University

NCAA D-III (11)
Buena Vista University
Central College
Coe College
Cornell College
Grinnell College
Iowa Wesleyan College
Loras College
Luther College
Simpson College
University of Dubuque
Wartburg College

NAIA (12)
Ashford University
Briar Cliff University
Clarke College
Dordt College
Graceland University
Grand View University
Morningside College
Mount Mercy College
Northwestern College
Saint Ambrose University
Waldorf College
William Penn University

Other 4-Year (3)
Emmaus Bible College
Faith Baptist Bible College
Vennard College

KANSAS

NCAA D-I (3)
Kansas State University
University of Kansas
Wichita State University

NCAA D-II (5)
Emporia State University
Fort Hays State University
Newman University
Pittsburg State University
Washburn University of Topeka

NAIA (15)
Baker University
Benedictine College
Bethany College

Bethel College
Central Christian College
Friends University
Haskell Indian Nations University
Kansas Wesleyan University
McPherson College
Mid America Nazarene University
Ottawa University
Southwestern College
Sterling College
Tabor College
University of Saint Mary

Other 4-Year (2)
Barclay College
Manhattan Christian College

KENTUCKY

NCAA D-I (6)
Eastern Kentucky University
Morehead State University
Murray State University
University of Kentucky
University of Louisville
Western Kentucky University

NCAA D-II (4)
Bellarmine University
Kentucky State University
Kentucky Wesleyan College
Northern Kentucky University

NCAA D-III (5)
Berea College
Centre College
Spalding University
Thomas More College
Transylvania University

NAIA (12)
Alice Lloyd College
Asbury University
Brescia University
Campbellsville University
Georgetown College
Kentucky Christian University
Lindsey Wilson College
Midway University
St. Catharine College
Union College
University of Pikeville
University of the Cumberland

Other 4-Year (1)
Boyce College

LOUISIANA

NCAA D-I (12)
Grambling State University
Louisiana State University
Louisiana Tech University
McNeese State University
Nicholls State University
Northwestern State University
Southeastern Louisiana University
Southern University, Baton Rouge
Tulane University
University of Louisiana at Lafayette
University of Louisiana at Monroe
University of New Orleans

NCAA D-III (2)
Centenary College
Louisiana College

NAIA (6)
Dillard University
Louisiana State University-Alexandria
Louisiana State University-Shreveport
Loyola University
Southern University at New Orleans
Xavier University of Louisiana

MAINE

NCAA D-I (1)
University of Maine, Orono

NCAA D-III (11)
Bates College
Bowdoin College
Colby College
Husson College
Maine Maritime Academy
Saint Joseph's College
Thomas College
University of Maine, Farmington
University of Maine at Presque Isle
University of New England
University of Southern Maine

MARYLAND

NCAA D-I (9)
Coppin State College
Loyola College
Morgan State University

Mount St. Mary's College
Towson University
U.S. Naval Academy
Univ. of Maryland, Baltimore County
Univ. of Maryland, College Park
Univ. of Maryland, Eastern Shore

NCAA D-II (1)
Bowie State University

NCAA D-III (10)
Notre Dame of Maryland
Frostburg State University
Goucher College
Hood College
Johns Hopkins University
McDaniel College
Salisbury University
St. Mary's College of Maryland
Stevenson College
Washington College

NAIA (1)
Washington Adventist University

MASSACHUSETTS

NCAA D-I (6)
Boston College
Boston University
College of the Holy Cross
Harvard University
Northeastern University
University of Massachusetts, Amherst

NCAA D-II (6)
American International College
Assumption College
Bentley College
Merrimack College
Stonehill College
University of Massachusetts at Lowell

NCAA D-III (45)
Amherst College
Anna Maria College
Babson College
Bay Path College
Becker College
Brandeis University
Bridgewater State College
Clark University (Massachusetts)
Curry College

Eastern Nazarene College
Elms College
Emerson College
Emmanuel College (Massachusetts)
Endicott College
Fitchburg State College
Framingham State College
Gordon College
Lasell College
Lesley University
Massachusetts College of Liberal Arts
Massachusetts Institute of Technology
Massachusetts Maritime Academy
Mount Holyoke College
Mount Ida College
Newbury College
Nichols College
Pine Manor College
Regis College (Massachusetts)
Salem State College
Simmons College
Smith College
Springfield College
Suffolk University
Tufts University
University of Massachusetts, Boston
University of Massachusetts, Dartmouth
Wellesley College
Wentworth Institute of Technology
Western New England College
Westfield State College
Wheaton College (Massachusetts)
Wheelock College
Williams College
Worcester Polytechnic Institute
Worcester State College

NAIA (1)
Fisher College

MICHIGAN

NCAA D-I (7)
Central Michigan University
Eastern Michigan University
Michigan State University
Oakland University
University of Detroit Mercy
University of Michigan
Western Michigan University

NCAA D-II (9)
Ferris State University
Grand Valley State University
Hillsdale College
Lake Superior State University
Michigan Technological University
Northern Michigan University
Northwood University
Saginaw Valley State University
Wayne State University

NCAA D-III (8)
Adrian College
Albion College
Alma College
Calvin College
Finlandia University
Hope College
Kalamazoo College
Olivet College

NAIA (11)
Aquinas College
Concordia University
Cornerstone University
Davenport University
Lawrence Technological University
Madonna University
Marygrove College
Rochester College
Siena Heights University
Spring Arbor University
University of Michigan-Dearborn

Other 4-Year (2)
Grace Bible College
Great Lake Christian College

MINNESOTA

NCAA D-I (1)
University of Minnesota, Twin Cities

NCAA D-II (9)
Bemidji State University
Concordia University, St. Paul
Minnesota State University Mankato
Minnesota State University Moorhead
Southwest Minnesota State University
St. Cloud State University
University of Minnesota Duluth
University of Minnesota, Crookston
Winona State University

NCAA D-III (20)
Augsburg College
Bethany Lutheran College
Bethel University
Carleton College
College of St. Benedict
St. Catherine University
College of St. Scholastica
Concordia College, Morehead
Crown College
Gustavus Adolphus College
Hamline University
Macalester College
Martin Luther College
North Central University
University of Northwestern, St. Paul
Saint Mary's University of Minnesota
St. John's University
St. Olaf College
University of Minnesota, Morris
University of St. Thomas

Other 4-Year (3)
Crossroads College
Oak Hills Christian College
Pillsbury Baptist Bible College

MISSISSIPPI

NCAA D-I (6)
Alcorn State University
Jackson State University
Mississippi State University
Mississippi Valley State University
University of Mississippi
University of Southern Mississippi

NCAA D-II (1)
Delta State University

NCAA D-III (3)
Millsaps College
Mississippi College
Rust College

NAIA (3)
Blue Mountain College
Tougaloo College
William Carey College

MISSOURI

NCAA D-I (5)
Missouri State University

Saint Louis University
Southeast Missouri State University
University of Missouri, Columbia
University of Missouri, Kansas City

NCAA D-II (14)
Drury University
Lincoln University
Lindenwood University
Maryville University of Saint Louis
Missouri Southern State Univ.-Joplin
Missouri University of Science & Tech.
Missouri Western State College
Northwest Missouri State University
Rockhurst University
Southwest Baptist University
Truman State University
University of Central Missouri
University of Missouri, St. Louis
William Jewell College

NCAA D-III (5)
Fontbonne University
Washington University
Webster University
Westminster College

NAIA (14)
Avila University
Central Methodist College
College of the Ozarks
Columbia College
Culver-Stockton College
Evangel University
Hannibal-LaGrange University
Harris-Stowe State University
Missouri Baptist University
Missouri Valley College
Park University
Saint Louis College of Pharmacy
Stephens College
William Woods University

Other 4-Year (8)
Baptist Bible College
Calvary Bible College
Central Bible College
Central Christian College of the Bible
Concordia Seminary - St. Louis
Ozark Christian College
St. Louis Christian College

MONTANA

NCAA D-I (2)
Montana State University-Bozeman
University of Montana

NCAA D-II (1)
Montana State University-Billings

NAIA (6)
Carroll College
Montana State University-Northern
Montana Tech of the Univ. of Montana
Rocky Mountain College
University of Great Falls
University of Montana-Western

Other 4-Year (1)
Salish Kootenai College

NEBRASKA

NCAA D-I (2)
Creighton University
University of Nebraska, Lincoln

NCAA D-II (4)
Chadron State College
University of Nebraska at Kearney
University of Nebraska at Omaha
Wayne State College

NCAA D-III (1)
Nebraska Wesleyan University

NAIA (9)
Bellevue University
College of Saint Mary
Concordia University
Doane College
Hastings College
Midland University
Nebraska Wesleyan University
Peru State College
York College

Other 4-Year (4)
Grace University
Nebraska Christian College
Nebraska University of Tech. Agriculture
Union College

NEVADA

NCAA D-I (2)
University of Nevada, Reno
University of Nevada, Las Vegas

NAIA (1)
Sierra Nevada College

NEW HAMPSHIRE

NCAA D-I (2)
Dartmouth College
University of New Hampshire

NCAA D-II (3)
Franklin Pierce College
Saint Anselm College
Southern New Hampshire University

NCAA D-III (6)
Colby-Sawyer College
Daniel Webster College
Keene State College
New England College
Plymouth State University
Rivier University

Other 4-Year (2)
Hesser College
New Hampshire Technical Institute

NEW JERSEY

NCAA D-I (8)
Fairleigh Dickinson University,
    Metropolitan Campus
Monmouth University
New Jersey Institute of Technology
Princeton University
Rider University
Rutgers, New Brunswick
Seton Hall University
St. Peter's College

NCAA D-II (4)
Bloomfield College
Caldwell College
Felician College
Georgian Court College

NCAA D-III (15)
Centenary College
College of Saint Elizabeth
Drew University
Fairleigh Dickinson University, Madison
Kean University
Montclair State University
New Jersey City University

Ramapo College
Richard Stockton College
Rowan University
Rutgers, Camden
Rutgers, Newark
Stevens Institute of Technology
The College of New Jersey
William Paterson University

NEW MEXICO

NCAA D-I (2)
New Mexico State University
University of New Mexico

NCAA D-II (3)
Eastern New Mexico University
New Mexico Highlands University
Western New Mexico University

NAIA (2)
Northern New Mexico College
University of the Southwest

Other 4-Year (2)
College of Santa Fe
Dine College

NEW YORK

NCAA D-I (22)
Binghamton University
Canisius College
Colgate University
Columbia University-Barnard College
Cornell University
Fordham University
Hofstra University
Iona College
Long Island Univ.-Brooklyn Campus
Manhattan College
Marist College
Niagara University
Siena College
St. Bonaventure University
St. Francis College, Brooklyn
St. John's University
Stony Brook University
Syracuse University
U.S. Military Academy
University at Albany
University at Buffalo
Wagner College

NCAA D-II (16)
Adelphi University
College of Saint Rose
Concordia College
Daemen College
Dominican College
Dowling College
Le Moyne College
Long Island University - Post Campus
Mercy College
Molloy College
New York Institute of Technology
Nyack College
Pace University
Queens College
Roberts Wesleyan College
St. Thomas Aquinas College

NCAA D-III (68)
Alfred State College
Alfred University
Bard College
Baruch College (CUNY)
Brooklyn College (CUNY)
Buffalo State College (SUNY)
Cazenovia College
Clarkson University
College of Brockport (SUNY)
College of Mount St. Vincent
College of New Rochelle
College of Staten Island (CUNY)
D'Youville College
Elmira College
Farmingdale State College
Hamilton College
Hartwick College
Hilbert College
Hobart and William Smith Colleges
Houghton College
Hunter College (CUNY)
Ithaca College
John Jay College (CUNY)
Keuka College
Lehman College (CUNY)
Manhattanville College
Medaille College
Medgar Evers College (CUNY)
Morrisville State College
Mount St. Mary College
Nazareth College

NY City College of Technology (CUNY)
New York University
Plattsburgh State University (SUNY)
Purchase College (SUNY)
Rensselaer Polytechnic Institute
Rochester Institute of Technology
Russell Sage College
The Sage Colleges
Sarah Lawrence College
Skidmore College
St. John Fisher College
St. Joseph's College (Brooklyn)
St. Joseph's College (Long Island)
St. Lawrence University
State Univ. College at Cobleskill
State Univ. College at Cortland
State Univ. of New York at Fredonia
State Univ. of New York at Geneseo
State Univ. College at New Paltz
State Univ. College at Old Westbury
State Univ. College at Oneonta
SUNY, Canton
SUNY, Farmingdale
SUNY, Morrisville
SUNY, Oswego
SUNY, Potsdam
SUNY Polytechnic Institute
SUNY, Maritime College
The City College of New York
U.S. Merchant Marine Academy
Union College
University of Rochester
Utica College
Vassar College
Wells College
Yeshiva University
York College

NAIA (1)
State Univ. College of Tech. at Delhi

Other 4-Year (3)
Briarcliffe College
Davis College
St. Joseph's College - Brooklyn

NORTH CAROLINA

NCAA D-I (18)
Appalachian State University
Campbell University
Davidson College

Duke University
East Carolina University
Elon University
Gardner-Webb University
High Point University
North Carolina A&T State University
North Carolina Central University
North Carolina State University
Univ. of North Carolina, Asheville
Univ. of North Carolina, Chapel Hill
Univ. of North Carolina, Charlotte
Univ. of North Carolina, Greensboro
Univ. of North Carolina, Wilmington
Wake Forest University
Western Carolina University

NCAA D-II (21)
Barton College
Belmont Abbey College
Brevard College
Catawba College
Chowan College
Elizabeth City State University
Fayetteville State University
Johnson C. Smith University
Lees-McRae College
Lenoir-Rhyne College
Livingstone College
Mars Hill College
University of Mount Olive
Pfeiffer University
Queens University of Charlotte
Shaw University
St. Andrews Presbyterian College
St. Augustine's University
University of North Carolina, Pembroke
Wingate University
Winston-Salem State University

NCAA D-III (7)
Greensboro College
Guilford College
Meredith College
Methodist College
North Carolina Wesleyan College
William Peace University
Salem College

NAIA (2)
Montreat College
St. Andrew's University

Other 4-Year (4)
Bennett College
Piedmont Baptist College
Roanoke Bible College
Warren Wilson College

NCAA D-II (2)
North Dakota State University
University of North Dakota

NCAA D-III (3)
University of Mary
Minot State University

NAIA (4)
Dickinson State University
Mayville State University
University of Jamestown
Valley City State University

Other 4-Year (1)
Trinity Bible College

OHIO

NCAA D-I (13)
Bowling Green State University
Cleveland State University
Kent State University
Miami University
Ohio State University
Ohio University
University of Akron
University of Cincinnati
University of Dayton
University of Toledo
Wright State University
Xavier University
Youngstown State University

NCAA D-II (12)
Ashland University
Cedarville University
Central State University
Lake Erie College
Malone College
Notre Dame College
Ohio Dominican University
Tiffin University
University of Findlay
Urbana University
Ursuline College
Walsh University

NCAA D-III (22)
Baldwin-Wallace College
Bluffton College
Capital University
Case Western Reserve University
College of Mount St. Joseph
College of Wooster
Defiance College
Denison University
Franciscan University of Steubenville
Heidelberg College
Hiram College
John Carroll University
Kenyon College
Marietta College
University of Mount Union
Muskingum University
Oberlin College
Ohio Northern University
Ohio Wesleyan University
Otterbein College
Wilmington College
Wittenberg University

NAIA (7)
Cincinnati Christian University
Lourdes University
Mount Vernon Nazarene University
Shawnee State University
University of Northwestern Ohio
University of Rio Grande
Wilberforce University

Other 4-Year (13)
Miami University - Hamilton
Miami University - Middletown
Ohio Christian College
Ohio State University - Lima
Ohio State University - Marion
Ohio State University - Newark
Ohio University - Chillicothe
Ohio University - Eastern
Ohio University - Lancaster
Ohio University - Zanesville
Southern State Community College
University of Akron - Wayne
University of Cincinnati - Clermont

OKLAHOMA

NCAA D-I (4)
Oklahoma State University
Oral Roberts University
University of Oklahoma
University of Tulsa

NCAA D-II (12)
Cameron University
East Central University
Northwestern Oklahoma State Univ.
Northeastern State University
Oklahoma Baptist University
Oklahoma Christian University
Oklahoma Panhandle State University
Rogers State University
Southeastern Oklahoma State Univ.
Southern Nazarene University
Southwestern Oklahoma State Univ.
University of Central Oklahoma

NAIA (8)
Bacone College
Langston University
Mid-America Christian University
Oklahoma City University
Oklahoma Wesleyan University
Saint Gregory's University
Southwestern Christian University
Univ. of Science and Arts of Oklahoma

Other 4-Year (2)
Hillsdale Free Will Baptist College
Rhema Bible College

OREGON

NCAA D-I (4)
Oregon State University
Portland State University
University of Oregon
University of Portland

NCAA D-II (2)
Concordia University
Western Oregon University

NCAA D-III (5)
George Fox University
Lewis and Clark College

Linfield College
Pacific University (Oregon)
Willamette University

NAIA (7)
Corban College
Eastern Oregon University
Multnomah University
Northwest Christian College
Oregon Institute of Technology
Southern Oregon University
Warner Pacific College

Other 4-Year (2)
Eugene Bible College
Multnomah Bible College

PENNSYLVANIA

NCAA D-I (14)
Bucknell University
Drexel University
Duquesne University
La Salle University
Lafayette College
Lehigh University
Pennsylvania State University
Robert Morris University
Saint Francis University (Pennsylvania)
Saint Joseph's University
Temple University
University of Pennsylvania
University of Pittsburgh
Villanova University

NCAA D-II (23)
Bloomsburg Univ. of Pennsylvania
California Univ. of Pennsylvania
Cheney Univ. of Pennsylvania
Chestnut Hill College
Clarion Univ. of Pennsylvania
East Stroudsburg Univ. of Pennsylvania
Edinboro Univ. of Pennsylvania
Gannon University
Holy Family University
Indiana University of Pennsylvania
Kutztown Univ. of Pennsylvania
Lincoln University
Lock Haven Univ. of Pennsylvania
Mansfield Univ. of Pennsylvania

Mercyhurst College
Millersville Univ. of Pennsylvania
Philadelphia University
Seton Hill University
Shippensburg Univ. of Pennsylvania
Slippery Rock Univ. of Pennsylvania
University of Pittsburgh, Johnstown
Univ. of the Sciences in Philadelphia
West Chester Univ. of Pennsylvania

NCAA D-III (59)
Albright College
Allegheny College
Alvernia College
Arcadia University
Baptist Bible College
Bryn Athyn College
Bryn Mawr College
Cabrini College
Carin University
Carnegie Mellon University
Cedar Crest College
Chatham College
Delaware Valley College
DeSales University
Dickinson College
Eastern University
Elizabethtown College
Franklin & Marshall College
Geneva College
Gettysburg College
Grove City College
Gwynedd-Mercy College
Haverford College
Immaculata University
Juniata College
Keystone College
King's College
La Roche College
Lancaster Bible College
Lebanon Valley College
Lycoming College
Marywood University
Messiah College
Misericordia University
Moravian College
Mount Aloysius College
Muhlenberg College
Neumann College

PSU - Altoona
PSU - Berks
PSU - Erie, the Behrend College
PSU - Harrisburg
Rosemont College
Saint Vincent College
Susquehanna University
Swarthmore College
Thiel College
University of Pittsburgh, Bradford
University of Pittsburgh, Greensburg
University of Scranton
University of Valley Forge
Ursinus College
Washington and Jefferson College
Waynesburg College
Westminster College
Widener University
Wilkes University
Wilson College
York College

NAIA (2)
Carlow College
Point Park University

Other 4-Year (15)
PSU - Abington
PSU - Brandywine
PSU - Beaver
PSU - Dubois
PSU - Fayette
PSU - Greater Allegheny
PSU - Hazelton
PSU - Lehigh Valley
PSU - Mont Alto
PSU - New Kensington
PSU - Schuykill
PSU - Shenango
PSU - Wilkes-Barre
PSU - Worthington
PSU - York

RHODE ISLAND

NCAA D-I (4)
Brown University
Bryant College
Providence College
University of Rhode Island

NCAA D-III (5)
Johnson and Wales University
Rhode Island College
Roger Williams University
Salve Regina University
Southern Wesleyan University

SOUTH CAROLINA

NCAA D-I (12)
Charleston Southern University
The Citadel
Clemson University
Coastal Carolina University
College of Charleston (South Carolina)
Furman University
Presbyterian College
South Carolina State University
University of South Carolina, Columbia
University of South Carolina - Upstate
Winthrop University
Wofford College

NCAA D-II (12)
Anderson University (South Carolina)
Benedict College
Claflin University
Coker College
Converse College
Erskine College
Francis Marion University
Lander University
Limestone College
Newberry College
North Greenville College
University of South Carolina - Aiken

NAIA (5)
Allen University
Columbia College
Morris College
University of South Carolina - Beaufort
Voorhees College

SOUTH DAKOTA

NCAA D-I (2)
South Dakota State University
University of South Dakota

NCAA D-II (5)
Augustana College (South Dakota)
Black Hills State University

Northern State University
South Dakota School of Mines & Tech.
University of Sioux Falls

NCAA D-III (1)
Presentation College

NAIA (4)
Dakota State University
Dakota Wesleyan University
Mount Marty College
Presentation University

TENNESSEE

NCAA D-I (12)
Austin Peay State University
Belmont University
East Tennessee State University
Lipscomb University
Middle Tennessee State University
Tennessee State University
Tennessee Technological University
University of Memphis
University of Tennessee, Chattanooga
University of Tennessee, Martin
University of Tennessee, Knoxville
Vanderbilt University

NCAA D-II (10)
Carson-Newman College
Christian Brothers University
King University
Lane College
Lee University
LeMoyne-Owen College
Lincoln Memorial University
Trevecca Nazarene University
Tusculum College
Union University

NCAA D-III (3)
Maryville College (Tennessee)
Rhodes College
University of the South

NAIA (8)
Bethel College
Bryan College
Cumberland University
Freed-Hardeman University
Fisk University
Martin Methodist College

Milligan College
Tennessee Wesleyan College

Other 4-Year (3)
Crown College
Free Will Baptist Bible College
Johnson Bible College

TEXAS

NCAA D-I (21)
Baylor University
Houston Baptist University
Lamar University
Prairie View A&M University
Rice University
Sam Houston State University
Southern Methodist University
Stephen F. Austin State University
Texas A&M University, College Station
Texas A&M University, Corpus Christi
Texas Christian University
Texas Southern University
Texas State University-San Marcos
Texas Tech University
University of Houston
University of North Texas
University of Texas at Arlington
University of Texas at Austin
University of Texas at El Paso
University of Texas at San Antonio
University of Texas, Pan American

NCAA D-II (15)
Abilene Christian University
Angelo State University
Dallas Baptist University
Lubbock Christian University
Midwestern State University
St. Edward's University
St. Mary's University
Tarleton State University
Texas A&M International University
Texas A&M University-Commerce
Texas A&M University-Kingsville
Texas Woman's University
University of Texas - Permian Basin
University of the Incarnate Word
West Texas A&M University

NCAA D-III (16)
Austin College

Concordia University at Austin
East Texas Baptist University
Hardin-Simmons University
Howard Payne University
LeTourneau University
McMurry University
Schreiner University
Southwestern University (Texas)
Sul Ross State University
Texas Lutheran University
Trinity University (Texas)
University of Dallas
University of Mary Hardin-Baylor
University of Texas at Dallas
University of Texas at Tyler

NAIA (12)
Huston-Tillotson College
Jarvis Christian College
Our Lady of the Lake University
Paul Quinn College
Southwestern Assemblies of God Univ
Texas A&M University, Texarkana
Texas College
Texas Wesleyan University
University of Houston - Victoria
University of Saint Thomas Houston
Wayland Baptist University
Wiley College

Other 4-Year (1)
Dallas Christian College

UTAH

NCAA D-I (6)
Brigham Young University
Southern Utah University
University of Utah
Utah State University
Utah Valley University
Weber State University

NCAA D-II (1)
Dixie State University

NAIA (1)
Westminster College

VERMONT

NCAA D-I (1)
University of Vermont

NCAA D-II (1)
Saint Michael's College

NCAA D-III (7)
Castleton State College
Green Mountain College
Johnson State College
Lyndon State College
Middlebury College
Norwich University
Southern Vermont College

VIRGINIA

NCAA D-I (15)
College of William and Mary
George Mason University
Hampton University
James Madison University
Liberty University
Longwood University
Norfolk State University
Old Dominion University
Radford University
University of Richmond
University of Virginia
Virginia Commonwealth University
Virginia Military Institute
Virginia Polytechnic Institute & State University
Virginia Tech

NCAA D-II (3)
University of Virginia College at Wise
Virginia State University
Virginia Union University

NCAA D-III (20)
Averett University
Bridgewater College (Virginia)
Christopher Newport University
Eastern Mennonite University
Emory and Henry College
Ferrum College
Hampden-Sydney College
Hollins University
Lynchburg College
Mary Baldwin College
University of Mary Washington College
Marymount University (Virginia)
Randolph College
Randolph-Macon College

Roanoke College
Shenandoah University
Southern Virginia University
Sweet Briar College
Virginia Wesleyan College
Washington and Lee University

NAIA (1)
Bluefield College

Other 4-Year (2)
Apprentice School
Christendom College

WASHINGTON

NCAA D-I (5)
Eastern Washington University
Gonzaga University
Seattle University
University of Washington
Washington State University

NCAA D-II (4)
Central Washington University
Seattle Pacific University
St. Martin's College
Western Washington University

NCAA D-III (4)
Pacific Lutheran University
University of Puget Sound
Whitman College
Whitworth College

NAIA (4)
Evergreen State College
Northwest University
Trinity Lutheran College
Walla Walla University

Other 4-Year (1)
Puget Sound Christian College

WEST VIRGINIA

NCAA D-I (2)
Marshall University
West Virginia University

NCAA D-II (14)
Alderson-Broaddus College
Bluefield State College
Concord College
Davis and Elkins College
Fairmont State College

Glenville State College
Ohio Valley College
Salem International University
Shepherd College
University of Charleston (West Virginia)
West Liberty University
West Virginia University
West Virginia Wesleyan College
Wheeling Jesuit University

NCAA D-III (1)
Bethany College (West Virginia)

NAIA (1)
WV University Institute of Technology

Other 4-Year (1)
Appalachian Bible College

WISCONSIN

NCAA D-I (4)
Marquette University
University of Wisconsin, Green Bay
University of Wisconsin, Madison
University of Wisconsin, Milwaukee

NCAA D-II (1)
University of Wisconsin, Parkside

NCAA D-III (25)
Alverno College
Beloit College
Carroll University
Carthage College
Concordia University
Edgewood College
Lakeland College
Lawrence University
Maranatha Baptist Bible University
Marian University
Milwaukee School of Engineering
Mount Mary University
Northland College
Ripon College
St. Norbert College
University of Wisconsin, Eau Claire
University of Wisconsin, La Crosse
University of Wisconsin, Oshkosh
University of Wisconsin, Platteville
University of Wisconsin, River Falls
University of Wisconsin, Stevens Point
University of Wisconsin, Stout

University of Wisconsin, Superior
University of Wisconsin, Whitewater
Wisconsin Lutheran College

NAIA (2)
Cardinal Stritch University
Viterbo University

Other 4-Year (15)
Northland Baptist Bible College
University of Wisconsin, Baraboo
University of Wisconsin, Barron
University of Wisconsin, Fond du Lac
University of Wisconsin, Fox Valley
University of Wisconsin, Manitowoc
University of Wisconsin, Marathon
University of Wisconsin, Marinette
University of Wisconsin, Marshfield
University of Wisconsin, Richland
University of Wisconsin, Rock Cty
University of Wisconsin, Sheboygan
University of Wisconsin, Washington
University of Wisconsin, Waukesha
Silver Lake College

WYOMING

NCAA D-I (1)
University of Wyoming

APPENDIX B

Nat'l Governing Bodies & Organizations

All-American Collegiate Golf Foundation
555 Madison Avenue, 12th Floor
New York, NY 10022
212.751.5170

Amateur Athletic Union (AAU)
PO Box10000
Lake Buena Vista, FL 32830-1000
407.363.6170
www.ausports.org

American Baseball Coaches Ass'n
108 South University Avenue, Suite 3
Mt. Pleasant, MI 48858-2327
517.775.3300
www.abca.org

American College Test (ACT)
PO Box 414
Iowa City, IA 52243
319.337.1554
www.actstudent.org

American Collegiate Hockey Association
PO Box 866
Troy, MI 48099-0866
410.357.9878
www.achahockey.org

American Football Coaches Ass'n
5900 Old McGregor Road
Waco, TX 76712
254.776.5900
www.afca.com

American Junior Golf Association
2415 Steeplechase Lane
Roswell, GA 30076
770.998.4653
www.ajga.org

American Swimming Coaches Ass'n
2101 N. Andrews Ave., Suite 107
Ft. Lauderdale, FL 33311
800.356.2722
www.swimmingcoach.org

American Volleyball Coaches Association
1227 Lake Plaza Drive, Suite B
Colorado Springs, CO 80906
719.576.7777
www.avca.org

National Archery Association
1 Olympic Plaza
Colorado Springs, CO 80909
719.578.4576
www.usarchery.org

Nat'l Ass'n of Intercollegiate Athletic(NAIA)
6120 South Yale Avenue, Suite 1450
Tulsa, OK 74136
918.494.8828
www.naia.org

Nat'l Ass'n for Girls & Women in Sports
1900 Association Drive
Reston, VA 22901
703.476.3452
www.aahperd.org

National Collegiate Athletic Ass'n (NCAA)
PO Box 6222
Indianapolis, IN 46206-6222
800.638.3731
www.ncaa.org

Nat'l Federation of State HS Associations
P.O. Box 20626
Kansas City, MO 64195
816.464.5400
www.nfhs.org

National Junior College Athletic Ass'n
PO Box 7305
Colorado Springs, CO 80933
719.590.9788
www.njcaa.org

USA Baseball
3400 East Camino Campestre
Tucson, AZ 85716
520.327.9700 phone
www.usabaseball.com

USA Basketball
5465 Mark Dabling Boulevard
Colorado Springs, CO 80918-3842
719.590.4800
www.usabasketball.com

USA Boxing
1 Olympic Plaza
Colorado Springs, CO 80909
719.578.4506
www.usaboxing.org

USA Cycling, Inc.
1 Olympic Plaza
Colorado Springs, CO 80909
719.578.4581
www.usacycling.org

USA Gymnastics
201 South Capitol Avenue, Suite 300
Indianapolis, IN 46225
317.237.5050
www.usa-gymnastics.org

USA Hockey
1775 Bob Johnson Drive
Colorado Springs, CO 80906
719.576.8724
www.usahockey.com

USA Shooting
1 Olympic Plaza
Colorado Springs, CO 80909
719.578.4670
www.usashooting.com

USA Softball
2801 NE 50th Street
Oklahoma City, OK 73111
800.277.0071
www.usasoftball.org

USA Swimming
1 Olympic Plaza
Colorado Springs, CO 80909
719.578.4578
www.usa-swimming.org

USA Table Tennis
1 Olympic Plaza
Colorado Springs, CO 80909
719.578.4583
www.usatt.org

USA Team Handball
1903 Powers Ferry Road, Suite 230
Atlanta, GA 30339
770.956.7660 phone
www.usateamhandball.org

USA Track & Field
1 RCA Dome, Suite 140
Indianapolis, IN 46225
317.261.0500 phone
www.usatf.org

USA Volleyball
715 South Circle Drive
Colorado Springs, CO 80910-2368
719.228.6800
www.usavolleyball.org

USA Weightlifting
1 Olympic Plaza
Colorado Springs, CO 80909
719.578.4508
www.usaweightlifting.org

U.S. Diving
201 South Capitol Avenue, Suite 430
Indianapolis, IN 46225
317.237.5252
www.usdiving.org

U.S. Fencing Association
1 Olympic Plaza
Colorado Springs, CO 80909-5774
719.578.4511 phone
www.usfencing.org

U.S. Field Hockey Association
1 Olympic Plaza
Colorado Springs, CO 80909-5773
719.578.4567 phone
www.usfieldhockey.com

U.S. Figure Skating Association
29 First Street
Colorado Springs, CO 80906
719.635.5200
www.usfsa.org

U.S. Olympic Committee
1750 E Boulder Street
Colorado Springs, CO 80909
719.632.5551
www.usoc.org

U.S. Racquetball Association
1685 W Utah
Colorado Springs, CO 80904
719.635.5396
www.usra.org

U.S. Rowing Association
201 South Capitol Avenue, Suite 400
Indianapolis, IN 46225
800.314.4ROW
www.rowing.org

U.S. Sailing
Box 1260-15 Maritime Drive
Portsmouth, RI 02871
401.683.0800
www.ussailing.org

U.S. Ski & Snowboard Association
1500 Kearns Boulevard
Park City, UT 84060
435.649.9090 phone
www.ussa.org

U.S. Soccer Federation
1801 S Prairie Avenue
Chicago, IL 60616
312.808.1300 phone
www.us-soccer.com

U.S. Speedskating
PO Box 450639
Westlake OH 44145
440.899.0128
www.uspeedskating.org

U.S. Synchronized Swimming
201 S Capitol Avenue, Suite 901
Indianapolis, IN 46225
317.237.5700
www.usasynchro.org

U.S. Taekwondo Union
1 Olympic Plaza
Colorado Springs, CO 80909
719.578.4632
www.ustu.org

U.S. Tennis Association (USTA)
70 W Red Oak Lane
White Plains, NY 10604
914.696.7000
www.usta.com

U.S. Water Polo
1685 West Utah
Colorado Springs, CO 80904
719.634.0699
www.uswp.org

Women's Sports Foundation
Eisenhower Park
East Meadow, NY 11554
800.227.3988
www.womenssportsfoundation.org

Young American Bowling Alliance
5301 South 76th Street
Greendale, WI 53129-1192
414.423.3421
www.bowl.com